This book

belongs to

....

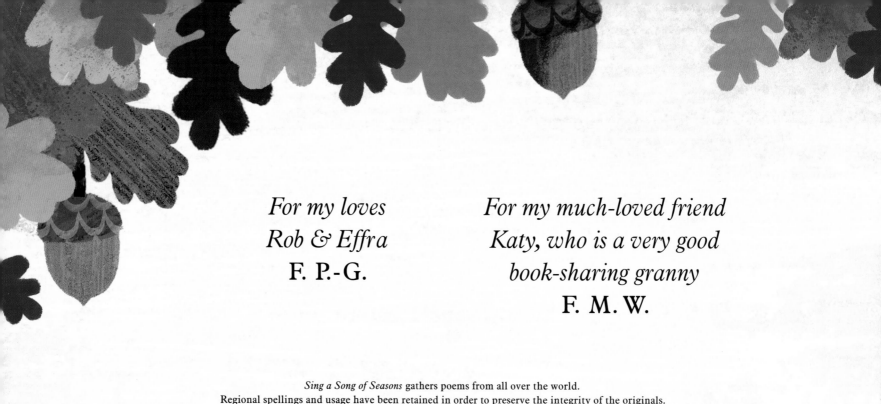

For my loves
Rob & Effra
F. P.-G.

For my much-loved friend
Katy, who is a very good
book-sharing granny
F. M. W.

Sing a Song of Seasons gathers poems from all over the world.
Regional spellings and usage have been retained in order to preserve the integrity of the originals.

Text compilation copyright © 2018 by Fiona Waters
Illustrations copyright © 2018 by Frann Preston-Gannon
Nosy Crow and its logos are trademarks of Nosy Crow Ltd. Used under license.
Copyright acknowledgments appear on pages 332–333.

First U.S. edition 2018

Library of Congress Catalog Card Number pending
ISBN 978-1-5362-0247-2

18 19 20 21 22 23 APS 10 9 8 7 6 5 4 3 2 1
Printed in Humen, Dongguan, China

This book was typeset in Aldine 721.
The illustrations were done in mixed media.

Nosy Crow
an imprint of
Candlewick Press
99 Dover Street
Somerville, Massachusetts 02144

www.nosycrow.com
www.candlewick.com

Sing a Song of Seasons

illustrated by
Frann Preston-Gannon

selected by
Fiona Waters

nosy crow

An imprint of Candlewick Press

CONTENTS

INTRODUCTION

For my seventh birthday, my parents gave me a book that—like this one—contained hundreds of poems. It was a small, fat book without pictures. At first I found it daunting: without pictures, there was nothing to catch my eye, nothing to lead me into the book.

But one rainy day after school, I took it down and began to read. And that was it for me: I fell in love with poetry, with rhyme, with rhythm, with the way that poetry squashed big feelings, big thoughts, big things, into tiny boxes of brilliance for the reader to unpack. It became my favorite book. I have it still. It is stuffed with little slips of paper that I used to mark the poems I liked best. As I grew older, those poems changed: a poem that baffled and bored me when I was seven revealed itself to me years later. I learned many of them by heart and could still recite them to you now.

At that time, I lived in a very small house with a very big yard on the outskirts of a city. The house was new, but had old trees around it — a lilac, a holly, and an apple tree so climbable it seemed as if it had grown itself with children in mind. Those trees were alive with small birds and, one spring, there was a nest with blue eggs in it and, later, three shockingly naked baby birds with gaping beaks that seemed to split their heads in two. Hedgehogs sometimes snuffled across the grass at night, and, one wet spring, I saw two frogs. There were daisies and dandelions and buttercups, and a flower so astonishingly complex and beautiful that I thought it must be magical. I later learned it was called a columbine. I spent hours in that yard, looking and learning.

I grew up. I read more poems. I became a publisher and, in my thirty years of publishing, I have published many poetry books. But none has been as ambitious as this one. My idea was to make a book as rich as the one I loved so much, but more beautiful and easier to find your way into. And I wanted, too, to make a book that helped you to pause and see the natural world around you.

I asked Fiona Waters to choose the poems and Frann Preston-Gannon to create the illustrations, so that each page became an invitation to draw the reader in.

You can read the poems on your own or share them. You can have them read to you or you can read them to someone else (poems come alive when they are read out loud). You can read the book from beginning to end quickly, or can read a poem every evening before you go to bed. You can dip into it, looking at only the poem chosen for your birthday, for example, and then close the book to think about that one poem. You can just look at the pictures. You can mark your favorite poems. You can learn some of the poems by heart, just for you to remember, or recite them out loud for a special person or a large crowd. You can keep it forever.

If you enjoy the book even half as much as we have enjoyed making it, then we will have done what we set out to do.

Kate Wilson
Publisher
Nosy Crow

JANUARY

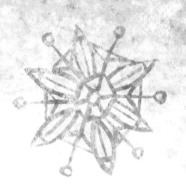

1st

THE GARDEN YEAR

January brings the snow,
Makes our feet and fingers glow.

February brings the rain,
Thaws the frozen lake again.

March brings breezes loud and shrill,
Stirs the dancing daffodil.

April brings the primrose sweet,
Scatters daisies at our feet.

May brings flocks of pretty lambs,
Skipping by their fleecy dams.

June brings tulips, lilies, roses,
Fills the children's hands with posies.

Hot July brings cooling showers,
Apricots and gillyflowers.

August brings the sheaves of corn,
Then the harvest home is borne.

Warm September brings the fruit,
Sportsmen then begin to shoot.

Fresh October brings the pheasant,
Then to gather nuts is pleasant.

Dull November brings the blast,
Then the leaves are whirling fast.

Chill December brings the sleet,
Blazing fire, and Christmas treat.

Sara Coleridge

2nd

THE NEW YEAR

The Young New Year has come so soon
I wonder where the Old Years go?
To some dim land behind the moon
Where starlight glimmers, pale and low.

And everything is grey and cold
And there they sit, those ancient years,
Their eyes so kind, and dim and old
Their faces lined with vanished cares.

Their voices rattle, dry like bones,
The while they talk of what has been,
And murmur in their hollow tones
Of all the triumphs they have seen.

While the Young Year, with earnest eyes,
Comes buoyant on, to run his race,
Nor dreams how fast his life-span flies
Nor how his end draws on apace.

Anonymous

3rd

JANUARY

January is
a clean white sheet, newly-ironed;
an empty page;
a field of freshly-fallen snow
waiting to be mapped
by our footsteps.

John Foster

4th

JANUARY

Little January
Tapped at my door today.
And said, "Put on your winter wraps,
And come outdoors to play."
Little January
Is always full of fun;
Today we coasted down the hill,
Until the set of sun.
Little January
Will stay a month with me
And we will have such jolly times—
Just come along and see.

Winifred C. Marshall

5th

BIRCH TREES

The night is white,
  The moon is high,
The birch trees lean
  Against the sky.

The cruel winds
  Have blown away
Each little leaf
  Of silver gray.

O lonely trees
  As white as wool . . .
That moonlight makes
  So beautiful.

John Richard Moreland

6th

STOPPING BY WOODS ON A SNOWY EVENING

Whose woods these are I think I know.
His house is in the village though;
He will not see me stopping here
To watch his woods fill up with snow.

My little horse must think it queer
To stop without a farmhouse near
Between the woods and frozen lake
The darkest evening of the year.

He gives his harness bells a shake
To ask if there is some mistake.
The only other sound's the sweep
Of easy wind and downy flake.

The woods are lovely, dark and deep.
But I have promises to keep,
And miles to go before I sleep,
And miles to go before I sleep.

Robert Frost

7th

DIAMOND POEM

Snow—
Soft flakes
Dust the street,
Painting pavements
A   brilliant   white.
In the lamp's light,
Glittering
Crystals
Gleam.

John Foster

8th

SNOWFLAKES

The snowflakes are falling
by ones and by twos;
There's snow on my jacket,
and snow on my shoes;
There's snow on the bushes,
and snow on the trees —
It's snowing on everything now,
if you please.

Leroy F. Jackson

9th

WINTER

Clouded with snow
The cold winds blow,
And shrill on leafless bough
The robin with its burning breast
Alone sings now.

The rayless sun,
Day's journey done,
Sheds its last ebbing light
On fields in leagues of beauty spread
Unearthly white.

Thick draws the dark,
And spark by spark,
The frost-fires kindle, and soon
Over that sea of frozen foam
Floats the white moon.

Walter de la Mare

10th

SNOWFLAKES

Sometime this winter if you go
To walk in soft new-falling snow
When flakes are big and come down slow

To settle on your sleeves as bright
As stars that couldn't wait for night
You won't know what you have in sight—

Another world—unless you bring
A magnifying glass. This thing
We call a snowflake is the king

Of crystals. Do you like surprise?
Examine him three times his size:
At first you won't believe your eyes.

Stars look alike, but flakes do not:
No two the same in all the lot
That you will get in any spot

You chance to be, for every one
Come spinning through the sky has none
But his own window-wings of sun:

Joints, points, and crosses. What could make
Such lacework with no crack or break?
In billion billions, no mistake?

David McCord

11th

WINTER DAYS

Biting air
Winds blow
City streets
Under snow

Noses red
Lips sore
Runny eyes
Hands raw

Chimneys smoke
Cars crawl
Piled snow
On garden wall

Slush in gutters
Ice in lanes
Frosty patterns
On windowpanes

Morning call
Lift up head
Nipped by winter
Stay in bed

Gareth Owen

12th

SNOW IN THE SUBURBS

Every branch big with it,
Bent every twig with it;
Every fork like a white web-foot;
Every street and pavement mute:
Some flakes have lost their way, and grope back upward, when
Meeting those meandering down they turn and descend again.
The palings are glued together like a wall,
And there is no waft of wind with the fleecy fall.

A sparrow enters the tree,
Whereon immediately
A snow-lump thrice his own slight size
Descends on him and showers his head and eyes,
And overturns him,
And near inurns him,
And lights on a nether twig, when its brush
Starts off a volley of other lodging lumps with a rush.

The steps are a blanched slope,

13th

A HARD WINTER

Not
a
twig
stirs.

The frost-bitten garden
huddles beneath
a heaped duvet of snow.

Pond,
tree,
sky
and
street

are granite with cold.

Wes Magee

14th

IN THE GARDEN

Greedy little sparrow,
Great big crow,
Saucy little tom-tits
All in a row.

Are you very hungry,
No place to go?
Come and eat my breadcrumbs,
In the snow.

Anonymous

15th

ONCE I SAW
A LITTLE BIRD

Once I saw a little bird
going hop, hop, hop.
So I cried, "Little bird,
will you stop, stop, stop?"
And was going to the window
to say, "How do you do?"
When he shook his tail
and away he flew.

Anonymous

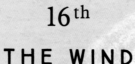

16th

THE WIND

I saw you toss the kites on high,
And blow the birds about the sky;
And all around I heard you pass,
Like ladies' skirts across the grass—
    O wind, a-blowing all day long,
    O wind, that sings so loud a song!

    I saw the different things you did,
    But always you yourself you hid.
    I felt you push, I heard you call,
    I could not see yourself at all—
        O wind, a-blowing all day long,
        O wind, that sings so loud a song!

        O you that are so strong and cold,
        O blower, are you young or old?
        Are you a beast of field and tree,
        Or just a stronger child than me?
           O wind, a-blowing all day long,
           O wind, that sings so loud a song!

Robert Louis Stevenson

17th

WHO HAS SEEN
THE WIND?

Who has seen the wind?
   Neither I nor you:
But when the leaves hang trembling,
   The wind is passing through.

Who has seen the wind?
   Neither you nor I:
But when the trees bow down their heads,
   The wind is passing by.

Christina Rossetti

18th

WHITE FIELDS

In winter-time we go
Walking in the fields of snow;

Where there is no grass at all;
Where the top of every wall,

Every fence, and every tree,
Is as white as white can be.

Pointing out the way we came—
Every one of them the same—

All across the fields there be
Prints in silver filigree;

And our mothers always know,
By the footprints in the snow,

Where it is the children go.

James Stephens

19th

A MORNING WALK

Over the land over the land
I walked at morn
Singing and trembling with cold

Southern Paiute song,
translated by John Wesley Powell

20th

SMALL, SMALLER

I thought that I knew all there was to know
Of being small, until I saw once, black against the snow,
A shrew, trapped in my footprint, jump and fall
And jump again and fall, the hole too deep, the walls too tall.

Russell Hoban

21st

Over wintry wind-whipped waves
The white-winged seagulls wildly sweep;
Weaving, winding, wheeling, whistling,
Where the wide waste waters weep.

Anonymous

22nd

SHELL

The sea fills my ear
With sand and with fear.

You may wash out the sand
But never the sound
Of the ghost of the sea
That is haunting me.

Ted Hughes

23rd

HERE WE GO ROUND THE MULBERRY BUSH

Here we go round the mulberry bush,
The mulberry bush, the mulberry bush,
Here we go round the mulberry bush,
On a cold and frosty morning.
This is the way we wash our hands,
Wash our hands, wash our hands,
This is the way we wash our hands,
On a cold and frosty morning.
This is the way we wash our clothes,
Wash our clothes, wash our clothes,
This is the way we wash our clothes,
On a cold and frosty morning.

Anonymous

24th

FLYING

I saw the moon,
One windy night,
Flying so fast—
All silvery white—
Over the sky
Like a toy balloon
Loose from its string—
A runaway moon.
The frosty stars
Went racing past,
Chasing her on
Ever so fast.
Then everyone said,
"It's the clouds that fly,
And the stars and moon
Stand still in the sky."
But I don't mind—
I saw the moon
Sailing away
Like a toy
Balloon.

J. M. Westrup

25th

STAR WISH

Star light, star bright,
First star I see tonight,
I wish I may, I wish I might,
Have the wish I wish tonight.

Anonymous

26th

THE STAR (EXTRACT)

Twinkle, twinkle, little star,
How I wonder what you are!
Up above the world so high,
Like a diamond in the sky.

Jane Taylor

27th

I SEE THE MOON

I see the moon,
And the moon sees me;
God bless the moon,
And God bless me.

Anonymous

31

28th

THE FURRY ONES

I like—
the furry ones—
the waggy ones
the purry ones
the hoppy ones
that hurry,

The glossy ones
the saucy ones
the sleepy ones
the leapy ones
the mousy ones
that scurry,

The snuggly ones
the huggly ones
the never, never
ugly ones . . .
all soft
and warm
and furry.

Aileen Fisher

29th

MAGGIE

There was a small maiden named Maggie,
Whose dog was enormous and shaggy;
    The front end of him
    Looked vicious and grim—
But the tail end was friendly and waggy.

Anonymous

33

30th

JANUARY

The days are short,
The sun a spark,
Hung thin between
The dark and dark.

Fat snowy footsteps
Track the floor.
Milk bottles burst
Outside the door.

The river is
A frozen place
Held still beneath
The trees of lace.

The sky is low.
The wind is gray.
The radiator
Purrs all day.

John Updike

31st

WINTER TIME

Late lies the wintry sun a-bed,
A frosty, fiery sleepy-head;
Blinks but an hour or two; and then,
A blood-red orange, sets again.

Before the stars have left the skies,
At morning in the dark I rise;
And shivering in my nakedness,
By the cold candle, bathe and dress.

Close by the jolly fire I sit
To warm my frozen bones a bit;
Or with a reindeer-sled, explore
The colder countries round the door.

When to go out, my nurse doth wrap
Me in my comforter and cap,
The cold wind burns my face, and blows
Its frosty pepper up my nose.

Black are my steps on silver sod;
Thick blows my frosty breath abroad;
And tree and house, and hill and lake,
Are frosted like a wedding-cake.

Robert Louis Stevenson

FEBRUARY

1st

WHEN SKIES ARE LOW
AND DAYS ARE DARK

When skies are low
and days are dark,
and frost bites
like a hungry shark,
when mufflers muffle
ears and nose,
and puffy sparrows
huddle close—
how nice to know
that February
is something purely
temporary.

N. M. Bodecker

2nd

SNOW TOWARD
EVENING

Suddenly the sky turned gray,
The day,
Which had been bitter and chill,
Grew soft and still.
Quietly
From some invisible blossoming tree
Millions of petals cool and white
Drifted and blew,
Lifted and flew,
Fell with the falling night.

Melville Cane

3rd

RED FOX

Red fox
   leaves a trail
      where he has stepped
this snowy morning
   leaving his
frozen scent nesting
   in the holes
of his paw prints

Coral Rumble

4th

FEBRUARY TWILIGHT

I stood beside a hill
   Smooth with new-laid snow,
A single star looked out
   From the cold evening glow.

There was no other creature
   That saw what I could see—
I stood and watched the evening star
   As long as it watched me.

Sara Teasdale

5th

SPELLBOUND

The night is darkening round me,
The wild winds coldly blow;
But a tyrant spell has bound me
And I cannot, cannot go.

The giant trees are bending
Their bare boughs weighed with snow,
And the storm is fast descending
And yet I cannot go.

Clouds beyond clouds above me,
Wastes beyond wastes below;
But nothing drear can move me;
I will not, cannot go.

Emily Brontë

6th

ON THE BEACH

The waves claw
At the shingle
Time after time.
They fall back
Again and again,
Sighing, sighing.

Michael Harrison

7th

THE WILD WHITE HORSES

The day they sent
The wild white horses into the sea
Didn't they frisk, and didn't they frolic there!
Didn't they set
Their wild white manes flying
Didn't they kick their legs up high in the air!

And night and day, night and day
Don't they pound along the shore,
Don't they thunder into the sand
and pound and pound again.

Oh, set them free, set them free
The wild white horses of the sea.

Berlie Doherty

8th

WINTER MORNING

Take one starry night
without cloud blankets.
Sprinkle icing sugar all about.
Leave to set.

Frosted leaves
sugared trees
spider's web appears
marked out in silver pen.

Serve with hats and mitts on,
boots and scarves on.
Scrape silver from the car.
Outside's a big fridge.

By dinner time the sun
you left it to bake in
has licked up all the sugar.
Winter's work's undone.

Angela Topping

9th

ICY MORNING HAIKU

On a frozen pond
a small dog is nervously
attempting to skate

Way up in the tree
a black cat grins with delight
watching and waiting

Beneath the clear ice
a big fish wonders if all
dogs walk on water

James Carter

10th

DUST OF SNOW

The way a crow
Shook down on me
The dust of snow
From a hemlock tree

Has given my heart
A change of mood
And saved some part
Of a day I had rued.

Robert Frost

11th

WHEN

In February there are days,
Blue, and nearly warm,
When horses switch their tails and ducks
Go quacking through the farm.
When everything turns round to feel
The sun upon its back—
When winter lifts a little bit
And spring peeks through the crack.

Dorothy Aldis

12th

WHITE SHEEP

White sheep, white sheep
  On a blue hill,
When the wind stops
  You all stand still.
You all run away
  When the winds blow;
White sheep, white sheep,
  Where do you go?

W. H. Davies

13th

THE MAN FROM MENINDEE

The man from Menindee was counting sheep,
He counted so hard that he went to sleep.
He counted by threes and he counted by twos,
The rams and the lambs and the wethers and ewes.
He'd counted six thousand, three hundred and ten,
But when he woke up, had to count 'em again!

D. H. Souter

14th

THAT'S WHAT
WE'D DO

If you were an owl,
And I were an owl,
And this were a tree,
    And the moon came out,
I know what we'd do.
We would stand, we two,
On a bough of the tree;
You'd wink at me,
And I'd wink at you;
That's what we'd do,
    Beyond a doubt.
I'd give you a rose
For your lovely nose,
And you'd look at me
    Without turning about.
I know what we'd do
(That is, I and you);
Why, you'd sing to me,
And I'd sing to you;
That's what we'd do,
    When the moon came out.

Mary Mapes Dodge

15th

OWL

A wise old owl sat in an oak,
The more he heard the less he spoke;
The less he spoke the more he heard.
Why aren't we all like that wise old bird?

Anonymous

16th

WINTER SCENE

There is now not a single
leaf on the cherry tree:
except when the jay
plummets in, lights, and,
in pure clarity, squalls:
then every branch
quivers and
breaks out in blue leaves.

Archie Randolph Ammons

17th

NIGHT OF WIND

How lost is the little fox at the borders of night,
Poised in the forest of fern, in the trample of wind!
Caught by the blowing cold of the mountain darkness,
He shivers and runs under tall trees, whimpering,
Brushing the tangles of dew. Pausing and running,
He searches the warm and shadowy hollow, the deep
Home on the mountain's side where the nuzzling, soft
Bodies of little foxes may hide and sleep.

Frances M. Frost

18th

SHINY

Shiny are the chestnut leaves
Before they unfold.
The inside of a buttercup
Is like polished gold.
A pool in the sunshine
Is bright too,
And a fine silver shilling
When it is new.
But the round full moon,
So clear and white,
How brightly she shines
On a winter night!
Slowly she rises,
Higher and higher,
With a cold clear light,
Like ice on fire.

James Reeves

19th

AFTERPEACE

This wind that howls about our roof tonight
And tears live branches screaming from great
    trees
Tomorrow may have scarcely strength to
    ruffle
The rabbit's back to silver in the sun.

Patrick McDonagh

20th

WINTER MORNING

Winter is the king of showmen,
Turning tree stumps into snow men
And houses into birthday cakes
And spreading sugar over lakes.
Smooth and clean and frosty white,
The world looks good enough to bite.
That's the season to be young,
Catching snowflakes on your tongue.
Snow is snowy when it's snowing,
I'm sorry it's slushy when it's going.

Ogden Nash

21st

THAW

The snow is soft,
and how it squashes!
"Galumph, galumph!"
go my galoshes.

Eunice Tietjens

22nd

SNOWMAN SNIFFLES

At winter's end
a snowman grows
a snowdrop
on his carrot nose,

a little, sad,
late-season sniff
dried by the spring
wind's handkerchief.

But day and night
the sniffles drop
like flower buds
—they never stop,

until you wake
and find one day
the cold, old man
has run away,

and winter's winds
that blow and pass
left drifts of snowdrops
in the grass,

reminding us:
where such things grow
a snowman sniffed
not long ago.

N. M. Bodecker

23rd

SNOW SPELL

This is our summer place

But the trees are bare
and all the leaves are crisp,
and the river that we paddled in
is slow and clinks with ice.
The air smokes from us
our voices echo thin and sharp as sleet
and everything is sleeping under snow.

In summer we were playing here,
we built a dam
my skimmer bounced six times
a wet dog ate our sandwiches
and Dad fell off the stepping stones
you swam your first five strokes.
The air was full of barks and laughs and shouts.

Not long ago, before the spell of snow.

Berlie Doherty

24th

TAM SNOW
(TO KAYE WEBB)

Who in the white wood
Barefoot, ice-fingered,
Runs to and fro?
        Tam Snow.

Who, soft as a ghost,
Falls on our house to strike
Blow after blow?
        Tam Snow.

Who with a touch of the hand
Stills the world's sound
In its flow?
        Tam Snow.

Who holds to our side,
Though as friend or as foe
We never may know?
        Tam Snow.

Who hides in the hedge
After thaw, waits for more
Of his kind to show?
        Tam Snow.

Who is the guest
First we welcome, then
Long to see go?
        Tam Snow.

Charles Causley

25th

ICICLES

We are little icicles
Melting in the sun.
Can you see our tiny teardrops
Falling one by one?

Anonymous

26th

Whether the weather be cold,
Or whether the weather be hot;
Whether the weather be fine,
Or whether the weather be not;
Whatever the weather
We'll weather the weather,
Whether we like it or not!

Anonymous

27th

SNOWY MOUNTAINS

I suppose you think Australia is all plains and white hot sun
Well, don't forget the mountains where the snowy rivers run,
Where the land is wild and rugged and, in winter, icy cold
And the people, like the country, are hardy, free and bold.

Snow gums grace the mountainside and tussock grass the flat
And men and horses work to rear the cattle sleek and fat.
In Springtime, Summer and Autumn, stock graze on that high plain
And before the Winter snow falls, they bring them down again.

Then the rivers, filled with melted snow, flow icy, deep and fast
One slip midstream on horseback may well be your last!
There are few things I like better than to ride a mountain track
And listen to a bird call as another echoes back.

The mountain song of currawong from treetops up on high,
And sulphur-crested cockatoos that screech across the sky,
The crystal Winter coolness of a Snowy Mountain morn
What a place to be alive . . . and glad that you were born!

Mike Jackson

28th

IN THE RAVINE

In the ravine   I stood
and watched the snowflakes
falling   into the stream
                    into the stream
flowing gracefully between
banks of snow
                    The black water
of the winter creek   came
around a bend   above
and disappeared
around a bend   below

Filled with melted snow
to the brim
the creek   came
around a bend—
and disappeared below
around a bend—
ground covered with snow

Thus I stood   the snow
descended   by degrees
into the stream
                    into the stream

W. W. E. Ross

29th

CALENDAR MONTHS

Thirty days hath September,
April, June, and November;
All the rest have thirty-one,
Excepting February alone,
Which has but twenty-eight days clear
And twenty-nine in each leap year.

Anonymous

MARCH

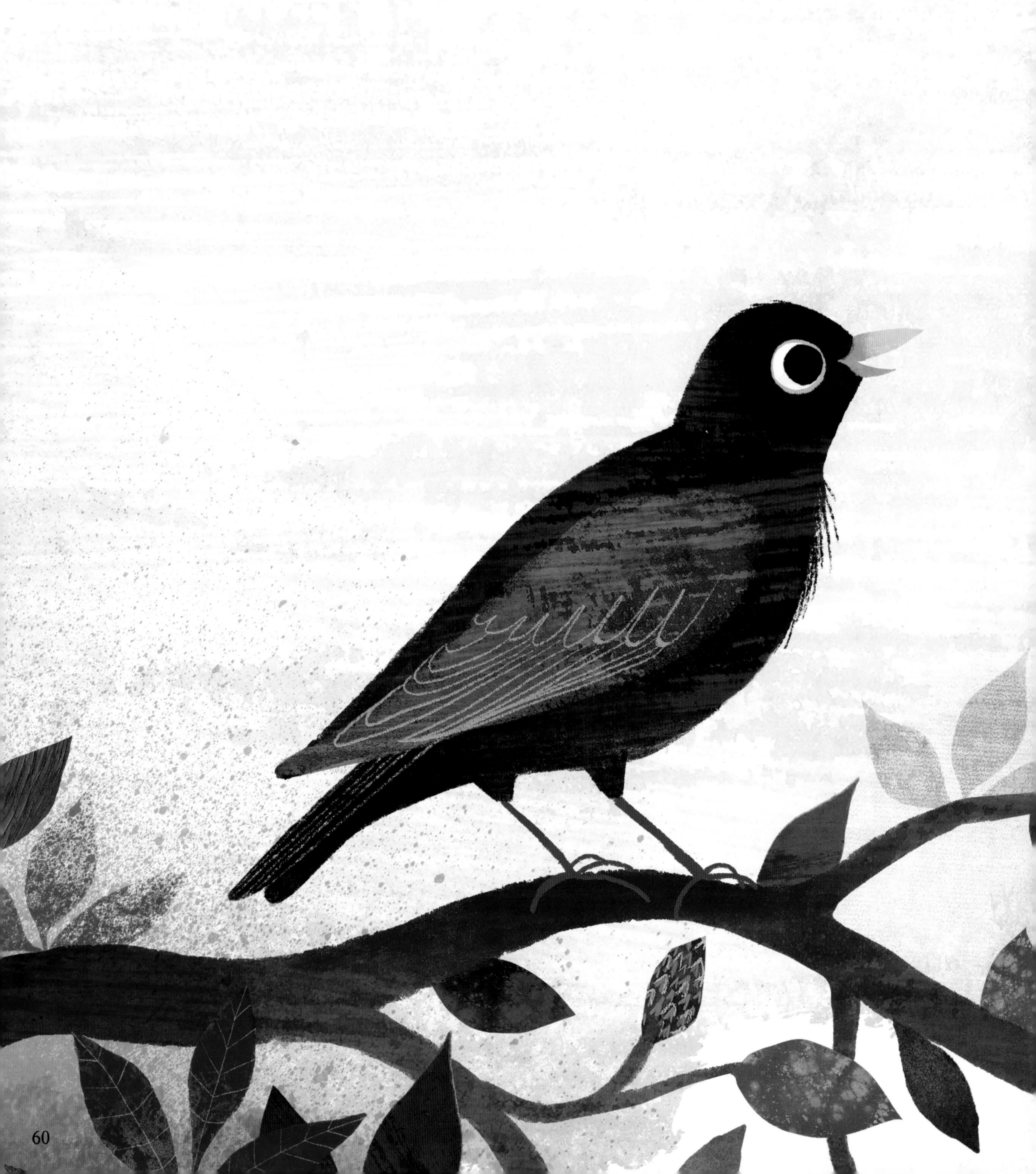

1st

I AM THE SONG

I am the song that sings the bird.
I am the leaf that grows the land.
I am the tide that moves the moon.
I am the stream that halts the sand.
I am the cloud that drives the storm.
I am the earth that lights the sun.
I am the fire that strikes the stone.
I am the clay that shapes the hand.
I am the word that speaks the man.

Charles Causley

2nd

PAPER DRAGONS

In March, kites bite the wind
and shake their paper scales.
They strain against their fiber chains
to free their dragon tails.

Susan Alton Schmeltz

3rd

SEASONS

Spring, summer, autumn, winter,
Every year the same—
Round and round the seasons go
Like a party game.
Spin the leaves from green to brown
Spin them on to gold,
Turn the weather up to hot
Turn it down to cold.
Chase the clouds across the sky
Paint a yellow sun,
Then the rain comes tumbling down
Spoiling all our fun.

Spring, summer, autumn, winter,
Every year the same—
Round and round the seasons go
Like a party game.

Steve Turner

4th

SEASONS

Spring is showery, flowery, bowery;
Summer: hoppy, croppy, poppy;
Autumn: wheezy, sneezy, freezy;
Winter: slippy, drippy, nippy.

Anonymous

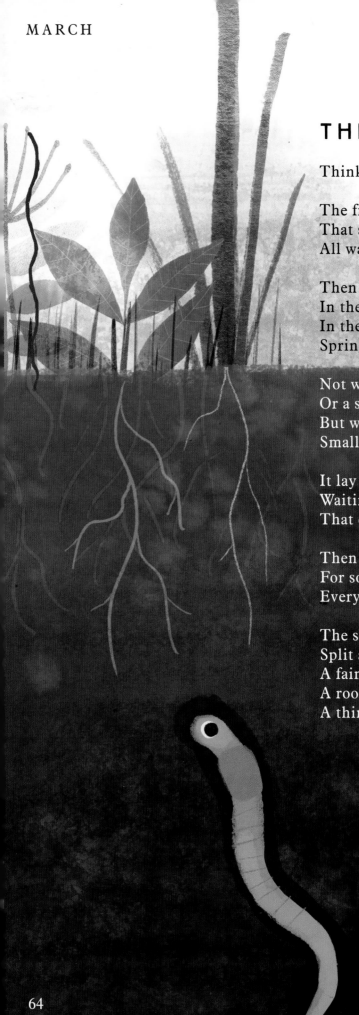

5th

THINK OF IT

Think of it

The first shudder of damp
That somehow signaled
All was ready

Then
In the deep inside of earth
In the muted underneath of winter
Spring began

Not with a sudden trumpet of green
Or a sky of confetti blossoms
But with a seed
Small, pale and barely breathing

It lay quietly
Waiting for the lavender clouds
That carry the first warm rains

Then
For some reason as ancient and
Everyday as the sun itself

The seed cracked
Split and softly burst into
A faint tendril
A root a sprout
A thin wisp of a growing thing

And
With no thought of stopping
It pushed through the
Dark soil with the force of
A billion winter winds
Until it

Pierced the crust of the outside and
Split the frozen armor of earth

Which has held spring safe
Since time began

Zaro Weil

6th

A SPIKE OF GREEN

When I went out
The sun was hot,
It shone upon
My flowerpot.

And there I saw
A spike of green
That no one else
Had ever seen!

On other days
The things I see
Are mostly old
Except for me.

But this green spike
So new and small
Had never yet
Been seen at all!

Barbara Baker

7th

Enjoy the earth gently
Enjoy the earth gently
For if the earth is spoiled
It cannot be repaired
Enjoy the earth gently

*Yoruba poem,
translator unknown*

8th

SPRING SONG

Spring is coming, spring is coming,
   Birdies, build your nest;
Weave together straw and feather,
   Doing each your best.

Spring is coming, spring is coming,
   Flowers are coming too;
Pansies, lilies, daffodillies
   Now are coming through.

Spring is coming, spring is coming,
   All around is fair;
Shimmer and quiver on the river,
   Joy is everywhere.

William Blake

9th

AFTER WINTER

A little bit of blowing,
    A little bit of snow,
A little bit of growing,
    And the crocuses will show!
On every twig that's lonely
    a new green leaf will swing,
On every patient tree-top
    a thrush will stop and sing.

A little bit of sleeting,
    A little bit of rain,
The blue, blue sky for greeting
    A snowdrop come again!
And every frozen hillside
    its gift of grass will bring,
And every day of winter
    another day of spring.

Carolyn Sherwin Bailey

10th

CAT AND CROCUSES

In the crocus-bed I saw her;
Like a queen enthroned she sat.
Yellow crocuses shone round her—
Royal, sun-illumined cat:

Orange eyes intensely lighted
By a vivid golden flame:
Fire of spring that burnt within her,
And in every flower the same.

World-surveying, world-contented,
Seated in her crocus-ring:
Cat and crocuses together
Basking in the fires of spring.

Eva Martin

11th

RABBIT

Lipperty Lipperty
Hoppity Hop
Whiffly Sniffly
Flippety Flop
Scritchety Scratchety
Twitchety Jump
Sniggly Snuggly
Jumpety Thump

Caryl Hart

12th

SPRING

Sound the Flute!
Now it's mute.
Birds delight
Day and Night.
Nightingale
In the dale
Lark in Sky
Merrily
Merrily Merrily to welcome in the Year

Little Boy
Full of joy.
Little Girl
Sweet and small.
Cock does crow
So do you.
Merry voice
Infant noise
Merrily Merrily to welcome in the Year

Little Lamb
Here I am,
Come and lick
My white neck.
Let me pull
Your soft Wool.
Let me kiss
Your soft face.
Merrily Merrily we welcome in the Year

William Blake

13th

Between the moon coming out
And the sun going in —
The red dragon-flies.

Nikyu, translated by R. H. Blyth

14th

THE DUCK

Behold the duck.
It does not cluck.
A cluck it lacks.
It quacks.
It is especially fond
Of a puddle or a pond.
When it dines or sups,
It bottoms ups.

Ogden Nash

15th

SIX LITTLE DUCKS

Six little ducks that I once knew,
Fat ones, skinny ones, they were too;
But the one little duck with
    the feathers on his back,
He ruled the others with his
    "Quack, quack, quack!
    Quack, quack, quack!"
He ruled the others with his
    "Quack, quack, quack!"

Down to the river they would go,
Wibble, wobble, wibble, wobble, to and fro;
But the one little duck with
    the feathers on his back,
He ruled the others with his
    "Quack, quack, quack!
    Quack, quack, quack!"
He ruled the others with his
    "Quack, quack, quack!"

Home from the river they would come,
Wibble, wobble, wibble, wobble, ho-hum-hum;
But the one little duck with
    the feathers on his back,
He ruled the others with his
    "Quack, quack, quack!
    Quack, quack, quack!"
He ruled the others with his
    "Quack, quack, quack!"

Anonymous

16th

RIDDLE

In marble walls as white as milk
Lined with a skin as soft as silk
Within a fountain crystal clear
A golden apple doth appear.
No doors there are to this stronghold
Yet thieves break in and steal the gold.

[An egg]

Anonymous

17th

TWO WRENS

Two wrens there were upon a tree:
Whistle and I'll come to thee;

Another came, and there were three:
Whistle and I'll come to thee;

Another came, and there were four.
You needn't whistle any more,

And there are none to show to you.
For, being frightened, off they flew.

Anonymous

18th

CROWS

I like to walk
And hear the black crows talk.

I like to lie
And watch crows sail the sky.

I like the crow
That wants the wind to blow:

I like the one
That thinks the wind is fun.

I like to see,
Crows spilling from a tree,

And try to find
The top crow left behind.

I like to hear
Crows caw that spring is near.

I like the great
Wild clamor of crow hate

Three farms away
When owls are out by day.

I like the slow,
Tired homeward-flying crow;

I like the sight
Of crows for my good night.

David McCord

19th

IN THE FIELDS

One day I saw a big brown cow
Raise her head and chew,
I said, "Good morning, Mrs. Cow,"
But all she said was, "Moo!"

One day I saw a woolly lamb,
I followed it quite far,
I said, "Good morning, little lamb,"
But all it said was, "Baa!"

One day I saw a dappled horse
Cropping in the hay,
I said, "Good morning, Mr. Horse,"
But all he said was, "Neigh!"

Anonymous

20th

PIPPA'S SONG

The year's at the spring;
The day's at the morn;
Morning's at seven;
The hillside's dew-pearled;
The lark's on the wing;
The snail's on the thorn;
God's in His heaven —
All's right with the world!

Robert Browning

21st

IF ONCE YOU HAVE SLEPT ON AN ISLAND

If once you have slept on an island
　　You'll never be quite the same;
You may look as you looked the day before
　　And go by the same old name,

You may bustle about in street and shop;
　　You may sit at home and sew,
But you'll see blue water and wheeling gulls
　　Wherever your feet may go.

You may chat with the neighbors of this and that
　　And close to your fire keep,
But you'll hear ship whistle and lighthouse bell
　　And tides beat through your sleep.

Oh, you won't know why, and you can't say how
　　Such change upon you came,
But— once you have slept on an island
　　You'll never be quite the same!

Rachel Field

22nd

WIND SONG

When the wind blows
The quiet things speak.
Some whisper, some clang,
Some creak.

Grasses swish.
Treetops sigh.
Flags slap
and snap at the sky.
Wires on poles
whistle and hum.
Ashcans roll.
Windows drum.

When the wind goes—
suddenly
then,
the quiet things
are quiet again.

Lilian Moore

23rd

MARCH WEATHER

Wind in pines
wind on water
wind in rushes
wind on feather

Sun in leaves
sun on loch
sun in reeds
sun on duck

Rain in trees
rain on river
rain in moss
rain on eider

All one morning
all together
in an hour
March weather

Tessa Ransford

24th

SILENT SONG

I find
A small, white egg
Under the conker tree
In the corner of the school field

I hold
The small, white egg
In the palm of my hand
And look up into the tangled branches

The tree
Is empty and the
Small, white egg
Is cold

I think
There is a song inside
The small, white egg
That we will never hear

Roger Stevens

25th

IF YOU FIND A LITTLE FEATHER

If you find a little feather,
a little white feather,
a soft and tickly feather,
    it's for you.

A feather is a letter
from a bird,
and it says,
"Think of me.
Do not forget me.
Remember me always.
Remember me forever.
Or remember me
at least
until
the little feather
is
lost."

So . . .

. . . if you find a little feather
a little white feather,
a soft and tickly feather,
    it's for you.
      Pick it up
        and . . .
            put it in your pocket!

Beatrice Schenk de Regniers

27th

BROOMS

On stormy days
When the wind is high,
Tall trees are brooms
Sweeping the sky.

They swish their branches
In buckets of rain
And swash and sweep it
Blue again.

Dorothy Aldis

26th

DAYFLIGHT

Thrushrush
Beakpoke
Stonestun
Snapsnail
Draindrop
Shellshed

Geoffrey Summerfield

28th

PIGEON AND WREN

Coo, coo, coo!
It's as much as a pigeon
  Can do
To bring up two!
But the little wren
  Can manage ten,
And bring them up
  Like gentlemen!

Anonymous

29th

FROGGIE, FROGGIE

Froggie, froggie.
Hoppity-hop!
When you get to the sea
You do not stop.
Plop!

Anonymous

30th

BLACK DOT

a black dot
a jelly tot

a scum-nail
a jiggle-tail

a cool kicker
a sitting slicker

a panting puffer
a fly-snuffer

a high hopper
a belly-flopper

a catalogue
     to make me

          frog

Libby Houston

31st

DAFFODILS

I wandered lonely as a cloud
That floats on high o'er vales and hills,
When all at once I saw a crowd,
A host, of golden daffodils;
Beside the lake, beneath the trees,
Fluttering and dancing in the breeze.

Continuous as the stars that shine
And twinkle on the Milky Way,
They stretched in never-ending line
Along the margin of a bay:
Ten thousand saw I at a glance,
Tossing their heads in sprightly dance.

The waves beside them danced, but they
Out-did the sparkling waves in glee:
A poet could not but be gay,
In such a jocund company:
I gazed — and gazed — but little thought
What wealth the show to me had brought.

For oft, when on my couch I lie
In vacant or in pensive mood,
They flash upon that inward eye
Which is the bliss of solitude;
And then my heart with pleasure fills,
And dances with the daffodils.

William Wordsworth

APRIL

1st

THE FIRST OF APRIL (EXTRACT)

The first of April, some do say,
Is set apart for All Fools' Day,
But why the people call it so
Nor I nor they themselves do know.

Anonymous

2nd

AFTER THE RAINS

After the rains,
when I opened my door
the spiders were at it
as hard as before,

mending their nets,
as the sun came again,
the patient, dependable
fly-fishermen.

N. M. Bodecker

4th

APRIL RAIN SONG

Let the rain kiss you.
Let the rain beat upon your head with silver liquid drops.
Let the rain sing you a lullaby.

The rain makes still pools on the sidewalk.
The rain makes running pools in the gutter.
The rain plays a little sleep-song on our roof at night—

And I love the rain.

Langston Hughes

3rd

THE RED WHEELBARROW

so much depends
upon

a red wheel
barrow

glazed with rain
water

beside the white
chickens

William Carlos Williams

5th

FIRST PRIMROSE

I saw it in the lane
One morning going to school
After a soaking night of rain,
The year's first primrose,
Lying there familiar and cool
In its private place
Where little else grows
Beneath dripping hedgerows,
Stalk still wet, face
Pale as Inca gold,
Spring glistening in every delicate fold.
I knelt down by the roadside there,
Caught the faint whiff of its shy scent
On the cold and public air,
Then got up and went
On my slow way,
Glad and grateful I'd seen
The first primrose of that day,
Half yellow, half green.

Leonard Clark

6th

Blow, breezes, blow!
Flow, rivers, flow!
Shine, sun, shine!
And grow, flowers, grow.

Anonymous

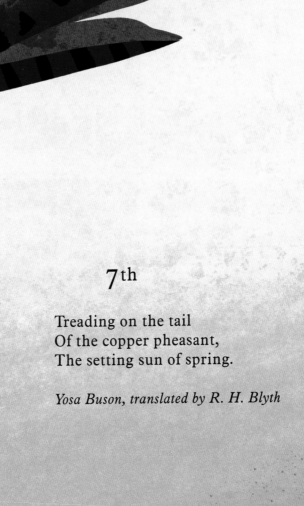

7th

Treading on the tail
Of the copper pheasant,
The setting sun of spring.

Yosa Buson, translated by R. H. Blyth

8th

WHEN A FISH . . .

When a fish
  screws
    slimy up
      out of
        the long
          dark
            river-
              downness
                and
                  bubbling
                    says
                      down
                        there
                          blub
                            in the
                              long
                                dark
                                  deepness
                                    blub
                                      there's
                                        an
                                          alli-
                                            gator
                                              blub
                                                oh
                                                  believe
                                                    that
                                                      fish.

Anonymous

10th

RIDDLE

Runs all day and never walks
Often murmurs, never talks.
It has a bed, but never sleeps;
It has a mouth but never eats.

[A river]

Anonymous

9th

Freckled fishes, flirting, flitting,
Flashing fast or floating free,
Flicking filmy fins like feathers,
Feeding from the flowing sea.

Anonymous

11th

I SOMETIMES THINK
I'D RATHER CROW

I sometimes think I'd rather crow
And be a rooster than to roost
And be a crow. But I dunno.

A rooster he can roost also,
Which don't seem fair when crows can't crow.
Which may help some. Still I dunno.

Crows should be glad of one thing though;
Nobody thinks of eating crow,
While roosters they are good enough
For anyone unless they're tough.

There're lots of tough old roosters though,
And anyway a crow can't crow,
So mebby roosters stand more show.
It looks that way. But I dunno.

Anonymous

12th

CHOOK,
CHOOK,
CHOOK

Chook, chook, chook, chook, chook,
Good morning, Mrs. Hen.
How many chickens have you got?
Madam, I've got ten.
Four of them are yellow,
And four of them are brown,
And two of them are speckled red,
The nicest in the town.

Anonymous

13th

CUCKOO

Cuckoo, cuckoo,
What do you do?
In April,
I open my bill;
In May,
I sing night and day;
In June,
I change my tune;
In July,
Away I fly;
In August,
Go I must.

Jane Taylor

14th

BIRDLAND

I can remember
The first time I flew.
The thrill of the take-off
The joy of the lift
The victory over gravity.
I so enjoyed
Cruising over clouds,
I so enjoyed
Looking out for angels,
How I enjoyed
Looking down
On the tiny people below
And wondering
If they were looking up at me
And wondering.

The birds were cool.
Flying is wonderful
And landing is exciting.
Yes I can remember
The first time I flew.
It was great.
I still fly
Every now and then
But now I use aeroplanes.

Anonymous

15th

FIVE LITTLE OWLS

Five little owls in an old elm-tree,
Fluffy and puffy as owls could be,
Blinking and winking with big round eyes
At the big round moon that hung in the skies:
As I passed beneath, I could hear one say,
"There'll be mouse for supper, there will, today!"
Then all of them hooted, "Tu-whit! Tu-whoo!
Yes, mouse for supper, Hoo hoo! Hoo hoo!"

Anonymous

16th

VOICES OF WATER

The water in the rain says
                    Tick Tick Tack
The water in the sleet says
                    Slush
The water in the ice says
                    Crick Crick Crack
The water in the snow says
                    Hush

The water in the sink says
                    Slosh Slosh
The water in the tap says
                    Drip
The water in the bath says
                    Wash Wash
The water in the cup says
                    Sip

The water in the pool says
                    Splish Splash
The water in the stream says
                    Trill
The water in the sea says
                    Crish Crash
The water in the pond . . .
                    stays still.

The water in the soil says
                    Sow, Sow
The water in the cloud says
                    Give
The water in the plant says
                    Grow, Grow
The water in the world says
                    Live

Tony Mitton

17th

FROG HOP

I may be ugly
but I have my hop.

I have no wish
to be kissed
and turned
to a prince
and mince
along
in awkward
finery.

Me? Abandon
my kingdom
of wet and weed
and insect feast?

Oh keep your kiss.
Oh keep your prince
dressed like a fop.

I'll keep my hop.

John Agard

18th

THE FROG

I saw a little frog,
He was cuter than can be,
He was sitting on a log
And I'm sure he croaked at me!

Anonymous

19th

THE TROUT

In the blue water
The trout wags its tail

*Southern Paiute song,
translated by John Wesley Powell*

20th

THE WIND

I can get through a doorway without any key,
And strip the leaves from the great oak tree.

I can drive storm-clouds and shake tall towers,
Or steal through a garden and not wake the flowers.

Seas I can move and ships I can sink;
I can carry a house-top or the scent of a pink.

When I am angry I can rave and riot;
And when I am spent, I lie quiet as quiet.

James Reeves

21st

THE STORM

See lightning is flashing,
The forest is crashing,
The rain will come dashing,
    A flood will be rising anon;

The heavens are scowling,
The thunder is growling,
The loud winds are howling,
    The storm has come suddenly on!

But now the sky clears,
The bright sun appears,
Now nobody fears,
    But soon every cloud will be gone.

Sara Coleridge

22nd

WHAT IS GREEN?

Green is the grass
And the leaves of trees
Green is the smell
Of a country breeze . . .

Green is a coolness
You get in the shade
Of the tall old woods
Where the moss is made.

Green is a flutter
That comes in Spring
When frost melts out
Of everything.
Green is a grasshopper
Green is jade
Green is hiding
In the shade—
Green is an olive
And a pickle.
The sound of green
Is a water-trickle.
Green is the world
After the rain
Bathed and beautiful
Again . . .

Green is the meadow,
Green is the fuzz
That covers up
Where winter was.
Green is ivy and
Honeysuckle vine.
Green is yours
Green is mine . . .

Mary O'Neill

23rd

THE WOODPECKER

The woodpecker pecked out a little round hole
And made him a house in the telephone pole.
One day when I watched he poked out his head,
And he had on a hood and a collar of red.

When the streams of rain pour out of the sky,
And the sparkles of lightning go flashing by,
And the big, big wheels of thunder roll,
He can snuggle back in the telephone pole.

Elizabeth Madox Roberts

24th

COUNTING-OUT RHYME

Silver bark of beech, and sallow
Bark of yellow birch and yellow
   Twig of willow.

Stripe of green in moosewood maple,
Color seen in leaf of apple,
   Bark of popple.

Wood of popple pale as moonbeam,
Wood of oak for yoke and barn-beam,
   Wood of hornbeam.

Silver bark of beech, and hollow
Stem of elder, tall and yellow
   Twig of willow.

Edna St. Vincent Millay

25th

THE FOAL

There's something new in the meadow:
it's soft, and brown and small
but its legs are long and straggly,
it can hardly stand at all.

The grey mare, gently breathing
there, in the lush, wet green,
has a new-born foal beside her
as limp as plasticine.

He rose, as we stopped to wonder,
and wobbled a little bit,
as if he were lately come to the world
and wasn't too sure of it.

Then he turned, and touched his mother,
searching her drowsed and dim
for the warm, sweet milk she carried.
What name shall we give to him?

Jean Kenward

26th

MARE

When the mare shows you
her yellow teeth, stuck
with clover and gnawed leaf,
you know they have combed
pastures of spiky grasses,
and tough thickets.

But when you offer her
a sweet, white lump
from the trembling plate
of your palm — she trots
to the gate, sniffs —
and takes it with velvet lips.

Judith Thurman

27th

SWAYBACKS IN THE SPRINGTIME

Two old horses, piebald swaybacks,
Mooching down by the chestnut trees:
Sharing a field in spring, though these
Are the winter days of their lives.

Two old horses, put out to grass here,
Suddenly break, frisk into a run
And their tough manes gleam in the rising sun
In the winter days of their lives.

Kit Wright

28th

WEATHER

It washes the floors off.
Then when it gets dry

You can sit in the park when the benches get dry
And you can walk on the street when it stops.

It's like a person who goes to do everything—
That's how the sky is.
The sky gets busy, she's working,
She's raining.
Then, when it stops raining, she doesn't do anything.
The sky is the sky,
And the sun comes out again.

Yetta Schmier

29th

CATCH A RAINBOW

If I could catch a rainbow

I'd hang it round your shoulders.
A rainbow scarf.
Its pot of gold
next to the beat of your heart.

If I could catch a rainbow

I'd make
rainbow puddles.
For you to splash colour
wherever your steps may take you.

If I could catch a rainbow

I'd turn it upside down.
A rainbow rocking bed
to let you float to a land of bliss,
drift safe on dozing dreams.

If I could catch a rainbow.

Brian Whittingham

30th

THE RAINBOW

Boats sail on the rivers,
    And ships sail on the seas;
But clouds that sail across the sky
    Are prettier far than these.

There are bridges on the rivers,
    As pretty as you please;
But the bow that bridges heaven,
    And overtops the trees,
And builds a road from earth to sky,
    Is prettier far than these.

Christina Rossetti

MAY

1st

ON MAY DAY

On May Day we dance,
On May Day we sing,
For this is the day
That we welcome the spring.

Anonymous

2nd

HOW WITHOUT ARMS

How, without arms,
did the sun
climb over the trees?

And without knees
to sink on,
how did it sink behind them?

And without eyes,
how did it peek
through the leaves?

And without
being wakened,
how did it rise?

JonArno Lawson

3rd

NEW DAY

The day is so new
you can hear it yawning,
listen:

The new day
is yawning
and stretching

and waiting to start.

In the clear blue sky
I hear the new day's heart.

Ian McMillan

4th

THE COCK CROWS
IN THE MORN

The cock crows in the morn
To tell us to rise,
And he that lies late
Will never be wise:
For early to bed,
And early to rise,
Is the way to be healthy
And wealthy and wise.

Anonymous

5th

A LITTLE TALK

The big brown hen and Mrs. Duck
Went walking out together;
They talked about all sorts of things —
The farmyard, and the weather.
But all I heard was: "Cluck! Cluck! Cluck!"
And "Quack! Quack! Quack!" from Mrs. Duck.

Anonymous

6th

TALL NETTLES

Tall nettles cover up, as they have done
These many springs, the rusty harrow, the plough
Long worn out, and the roller made of stone:
Only the elm butt tops the nettles now.

This corner of the farmyard I like most:
As well as any bloom upon a flower
I like the dust on the nettles, never lost
Except to prove the sweetness of a shower.

Edward Thomas

7th

THE FARMYARD

One black horse standing by the gate,
Two plump cats eating from a plate;
Three big goats kicking up their heels,
Four pink pigs full of grunts and squeals;
Five white cows coming slowly home,
Six small chicks starting off to roam;
Seven fine doves perched upon the shed,
Eight grey geese eager to be fed;
Nine young lambs full of frisky fun,
Ten brown bees buzzing in the sun.

A. A. Attwood

8th

SUMMER FULL MOON

The cloud tonight
is like a white
    Persian cat —

It lies among the stars
with eyes almost shut
lapping the milk from
the moon's brimming dish.

James Kirkup

9th

QUESTIONS AT NIGHT

Why
Is the sky?

What starts the thunder overhead?
Who makes the crashing noise?
Are the angels falling out of bed?
Are they breaking all their toys?

Why does the sun go down so soon?
Why do the night-clouds crawl
Hungrily up to the new-laid moon
And swallow it, shell and all?

If there's a Bear among the stars,
As all the people say,
Won't he jump over those pasture-bars
And drink up the Milky Way?

Does every star that happens to fall
Turn into a firefly?
Can't it ever get back to Heaven at all?
And why
Is the sky?

Louis Untermeyer

10th

BADGERS

Badgers come creeping from dark under ground,
Badgers scratch hard with a bristly sound,
Badgers go nosing around.

Badgers have whiskers and black and white faces,
Badger cubs scramble and scrap and run races,
Badgers like overgrown places.

Badgers don't jump when a vixen screams,
Badgers drink quietly from moonshiny streams,
Badgers dig holes in our dreams.

Badgers are working while you and I sleep,
Pushing their tunnels down twisting and steep,
Badgers have secrets to keep.

Richard Edwards

11th

DUCKS' DITTY

All along the backwater,
Through the rushes tall,
Ducks are a-dabbling,
Up tails all!

Ducks' tails, drakes' tails,
Yellow feet a-quiver,
Yellow bills all out of sight
Busy in the river!

Slushy green undergrowth
Where the roach swim —
Here we keep our larder,
Cool and full and dim!

Everyone for what he likes!
We like to be
Heads down, tails up,
Dabbling free!

High in the blue above
Swifts whirl and call —
We are down a-dabbling
Up tails all!

Kenneth Grahame

12th

THE TICKLE RHYME

"Who's that tickling my back?" said the wall.
"Me," said a small
Caterpillar. "I'm learning
To crawl."

Ian Serraillier

13th

THE YELLOW TULIP

For weeks
it struggled
through the hard crust
of the spring earth
and a foot
of air

Just to be
scorched
by the sun
jolted
by raindrops
blasted
by the wind

But on this gentle
May morning
as it opens
yellow petals
to the sky

Nothing else matters

George Swede

14th

THE CATERPILLAR

Brown and furry
Caterpillar in a hurry,
Take your walk
To the shady leaf, or stalk,
Or what not,
Which may be the chosen spot.
No toad spy you,
Hovering bird of prey pass by you;
Spin and die,
To live again a butterfly.

Christina Rossetti

15th

ONLY MY OPINION

Is a caterpillar ticklish?
    Well, it's always my belief
That he giggles, as he wiggles
    Across a hairy leaf.

Monica Shannon

16th

THE FROG

What a wonderful bird the frog are—
When he sit, he stand almost;
When he hop, he fly almost.
He ain't got no sense hardly;
He ain't got no tail hardly either.
When he sit, he sit on what he ain't got—almost.

Anonymous

17th

The little fish
Carried backwards
In the clear water.

*Takai Kito, translated
by R. H. Blyth*

18th

THE HERON

I said to the heron, "Why do you stand
In that swift-flowing stream in the pebbles and sand
On only one foot?
I'd have thought it would be more convenient to put
Both feet in the stream while you patiently seek
The silvery fish to spear with your beak?"

The heron glared back and his voice quickly rose,
"I'd have thought it was something that everyone knows:
In a warm, feathered hollow one foot I now hold
Because swift-flowing streams are excessively cold."

Gregory Harrison

19th

SNEEZING

Sneeze on Monday, sneeze for danger;
Sneeze on Tuesday, miss a stranger;
Sneeze on Wednesday, get a letter;
Sneeze on Thursday, something better;
Sneeze on Friday, sneeze for sorrow
Sneeze on Saturday,
    see your sweetheart tomorrow.

Anonymous

20th

O DANDELION

"O dandelion, yellow as gold,
What do you do all day?"

*"I just wait here in the tall green grass
Till the children come to play."*

"O dandelion, yellow as gold,
What do you do all night?"

*"I wait and wait till the cool dews fall
And my hair grows long and white."*

"And what do you do when your hair is white
And the children come to play?"

*"They take me up in their dimpled hands
And blow my hair away."*

Anonymous

21st

YELLOW WEED

How did you get here,
weed?
Who brought your seed?

Did it lift
on the wind and
sail
and drift
from a far and yellow
field?

Was your seed a
burr,
a sticky burr that
clung to a
fox's
furry tail?

Did it fly with a
bird
who liked to feed
on the tasty
seed
of the yellow
weed?
How did you come?

Lilian Moore

22nd

TREASURE

Judith goes to feed the hens
plaits down her back
legs bare in navy shorts
—the bucket's red.
Lifting the latch
of the wire mesh gate
she steps in the hen-run,
Rhode Island reds
rush in a tumbled fuss
of featherness
hustling for grain.

Six nesting-boxes
huddle in the shade
sheltered from sun
six eggs are laid
smudgy with mud
fuzzy with hen-down.

Carefully now
into the bucket
   one
      by
         one
dying to tell
longing to yell
but she mustn't run.
Tenderly now
past rhubarb and sage
by lupins and hollyhocks
"Nanna!" she calls.
"I've got them all
—an egg for every box!"

Una Leavy

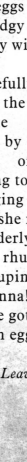

24th

THE POULTRIES

Let's think of eggs.
They have no legs.
Chickens come from eggs
But they have legs.
The plot thickens;
Eggs come from chickens,
But have no legs under 'em.
What a conundrum!

Ogden Nash

23rd

HEN'S SONG

Chick, chick, come out of your shell,
I've warmed you long and I've warmed you well;
The sun is hot and the sky is blue
Quick, chick, it's time you came through.

Rose Fyleman

25th

THE WAY THROUGH
THE WOODS

They shut the road through the woods
Seventy years ago.
Weather and rain have undone it again,
And now you would never know
There was once a road through the woods
Before they planted the trees.
It is underneath the coppice and heath,
And the thin anemones.
Only the keeper sees
That, where the ring-dove broods,
And the badgers roll at ease,
There was once a road through the woods.

Yet, if you enter the woods
Of a summer evening late,
When the night air cools on the trout-ringed pools
Where the otter whistles his mate,
(They fear not men in the woods,
Because they see so few.)
You will hear the beat of a horse's feet,
And the swish of a skirt in the dew,
Steadily cantering through
The misty solitudes,
As though they perfectly knew
The old lost road through the woods . . .
But there is no road through the woods.

Rudyard Kipling

26th

QUEEN ANNE'S LACE

Queen Anne, Queen Anne, has washed her lace
  (She chose a summer day)
And hung it in a grassy place
  To whiten, if it may.

Queen Anne, Queen Anne, has left it there,
  And slept the dewy night;
Then waked, to find the sunshine fair,
  And all the meadows white.

Queen Anne, Queen Anne, is dead and gone
  (She died a summer's day),
But left her lace to whiten on
  Each weed-entangled way!

Mary Leslie Newton

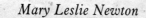

27th

WHISPERING LEAVES

I am wondering
what it is
the leaves are whispering to me.
Which language they speak.
It doesn't seem funny
but it might be.
It takes years
getting leaf ears
only there aren't
many quiet days
to sit out and learn
leaf talk.
Leaves, I'm listening.

Julie O'Callaghan

28th

BUTTERCUP

Buttercups gleam, bright butter gold,
buttercup, buttercup, buttercup-cup.

Buttercups, tall, rambling wild,
buttercup, buttercup, buttercup-cup.

Butterflies and daisies dancing in the meadow,
buttercup, buttercup, buttercup-cup.

Bare legs tickled by green and yellow,
buttercup, buttercup, buttercup-cup.

Buttercups singing the summertime tune,
buttercup, buttercup, buttercup-cup.

Buttercups close at the rise of the moon,
buttercup, buttercup, buttercup-cup.

Mandy Coe

29th

A BIRD CAME DOWN THE WALK

A bird came down the walk:
He did not know I saw;
He bit an angleworm in halves
And ate the fellow, raw,

And then he drank a dew
From a convenient grass,
And then hopped sidewise to the wall
To let a beetle pass.

He glanced with rapid eyes
That hurried all abroad,
They looked like frightened beads, I thought;
He stirred his velvet head

Like one in danger; cautious,
I offered him a crumb,
And he unrolled his feathers
And rowed him softer home

Than oars divide the ocean,
Too silver for a seam,
Or butterflies, off banks of noon,
Leap, plashless, as they swim.

Emily Dickinson

30th

FINDING MAGIC

Are you looking for magic?
It's everywhere.
See how a kestrel
Hovers in air;
Watch a cat move:
What elegant grace!
See how a conker
Fits its case.
Watch a butterfly come
From a chrysalis,
Or a chick from an egg—
There's magic in this;
Then think of the
Marvellous mystery
Of an acorn becoming
A huge oak tree.
There's magic in sunsets
And patterned skies:
There's magic in moonlight—
Just use your eyes!
If you're looking for magic
It's easily found:
It's everywhere,
It's all around.

Eric Finney

31st

MAY

Now children may
    Go out of doors,
Without their coats,
    To candy stores.

The apple branches
    And the pear
May float their blossoms
    Through the air,

And Daddy may
    Get out his hoe
To plant tomatoes
    In a row,

And, afterward,
    May lazily
Look at some baseball
    On TV.

John Updike

JUNE

1st

ALL IN JUNE

A week ago I had a fire,
   To warm my feet, my hands and face;
Cold winds, that never make a friend,
   Crept in and out of every place.

Today, the fields are rich in grass,
   And buttercups in thousands grow;
I'll show the World where I have been—
   With gold-dust seen on either shoe.

Till to my garden back I come,
   Where bumble-bees, for hours and hours,
Sit on their soft, fat, velvet bums,
   To wriggle out of hollow flowers.

W. H. Davies

2nd

BUTTERFLIES

Butterflies;
Like pieces of torn paper
Strewn into the wind.

N. C. Wickramasinghe

3rd

BEE! I'M EXPECTING YOU!

Bee! I'm expecting you!
Was saying Yesterday
To Somebody you know
That you were due—

The Frogs got Home last Week—
Are settled, and at work—
Birds, mostly back—
The Clover warm and thick—

You'll get my Letter by
The seventeenth; Reply
Or better, be with me—
Yours, Fly

Emily Dickinson

4th

BEDTIME (EXTRACT)

The evening is coming,
The sun sinks to rest;
The rooks are all flying
Straight home to the nest.
"Caw!" says the rook, as he flies overhead;
"It's time little people were going to bed!"

The flowers are closing;
The daisy's asleep;
The primrose is buried
In slumber so deep.
Shut up for the night is the pimpernel red;
It's time little people were going to bed!

The butterfly, drowsy,
Has folded its wing;
The bees are returning,
No more the birds sing.
Their labour is over, their nestlings are fed;
It's time little people were going to bed!

Thomas Hood

5th

BED IN SUMMER

In winter I get up at night
And dress by yellow candlelight.
In summer, quite the other way,
I have to go to bed by day.

I have to go to bed and see
The birds still hopping on the tree,
Or hear the grown-up people's feet
Still going past me in the street.

And does it not seem hard to you,
When all the sky is clear and blue,
And I should like so much to play,
To have to go to bed by day?

Robert Louis Stevenson

6th

There's no need to light a night light
On a light night like tonight;
For a night light's a slight light
On a light night like tonight.

Anonymous

7th

THE SEA

The sea is a hungry dog,
Giant and grey.
He rolls on the beach all day.
With his clashing teeth and shaggy jaws
Hour upon hour he gnaws
The rumbling, tumbling stones,
And "Bones, bones, bones, bones!"
The giant sea-dog moans,
Licking his greasy paws.

And when the night wind roars
And the moon rocks in the stormy cloud,
He bounds to his feet and snuffs and sniffs,
Shaking his wet sides over the cliffs,
And howls and hollos long and loud.

But on quiet days in May or June,
When even the grasses on the dune
Play no more their reedy tune,
With his head between his paws
He lies on the sandy shores,
So quiet, so quiet, he scarcely snores.

James Reeves

8th

BUSY BUGS

Out in the garden
look down low
see all the busy bugs
come and go

Wriggly bugs
that can't keep still

Tiny bugs
that build a hill

Shiny bugs
that feed on leaves

Spotty bugs
that climb up trees

Out in the garden . . .

Noisy bugs
that live in grass

Bouncy bugs
that move so fast

Crawly bugs
that hide in sand

Tickly bugs
that like your hand!

Out in the garden . . .

James Carter

9th

WORM WORDS

"Keep still!"
said Big Worm
to Little Worm.
"You're driving me
round the bend."

"Don't be daft,"
said Little Worm.
"I'm your other end."

Tony Mitton

10th

THE SONG OF A MOLE

All I did this afternoon was
Dig, dig, dig,
And all I'll do tomorrow will be
Dig, dig, dig,
And yesterday from dusk till dawn
I dug, dug, dug.
I sometimes think I'd rather be
A slug, slug, slug.

Richard Edwards

11th

THE SNAIL'S MONOLOGUE

Shall I dwell in my shell?
Shall I not dwell in my shell?
Dwell in shell?
Rather not dwell?
Shall I not dwell,
shall I dwell,
dwell in shell,
shall I shell,
shallIshellIshallIshellIshallI . . .?

(The snail gets so entangled with his thoughts
or, rather, the thoughts run away with him
so that he must postpone the decision.)

Christian Morgenstern, translated by Max Knight

12th

THE SNAIL

At sunset, when the night-dews fall,
Out of the ivy on the wall
With horns outstretched and pointed tail
Comes the grey and noiseless snail.
On ivy stems she clambers down,
Carrying her house of brown.
Safe in the dark, no greedy eye
Can her tender body spy,
While she herself, a hungry thief,
Searches out the freshest leaf.
She travels on as best she can
Like a toppling caravan.

James Reeves

13th

CABBAGE-BITE

FIND LEAF
EAT LEAF
LEAF MEAL
PIECEMEAL
LEAVELEAF
ALL HOLE

Geoffrey Summerfield

14th

MR. SNAIL

Quaint and quirky, never quick,
Mother Nature's glue-stick,
Hard shell, tacky tail,
Glue the garden, Mr. Snail.

Celia Warren

15th

SOLITUDE

How still it is here in the woods. The trees
    Stand motionless, as if they do not dare
    To stir, lest it should break the spell. The air
Hangs quiet as spaces in a marble frieze.
Even this little brook, that runs at ease,
    Whispering and gurgling in its knotted bed,
    Seems but to deepen with its curling thread
Of sound the shadowy sun-pierced silences.

Sometimes a hawk screams or a woodpecker
    Startles the stillness from its fixèd mood
With his loud careless tap. Sometimes I hear
    The dreamy white-throat from some far-off tree
Pipe slowly on the listening solitude
    His five pure notes succeeding pensively.

Archibald Lampman

16th

THE INTRUDER

Two-boots in the forest walks,
Pushing through the bracken stalks.

Vanishing like a puff of smoke,
Nimbletail flies up the oak.

Longears helter-skelter shoots
Into his house among the roots.

At work upon the highest bark,
Tapperbill knocks off to hark.

Painted-wings through sun and shade
Flounces off along the glade.

Not a creature lingers by,
When clumping Two-boots comes to pry.

James Reeves

17th

THE MOON

The moon is a boat that drifts in the sky
with nobody near but the stars that stand by
peering down as if they wished to say,
"Who pulled up the anchor and let you away?"

Iain Crichton Smith

18th

CAT

White as silk
the moon looks down at my cat.
My cat looks back
and ponders the leap.

Brian Morse

19th

IN THE BLUE NIGHT

How shall I begin my song in the
blue night that is settling?
I will sit here and begin my song.

Owl Woman (Tohono O'odham),
translated by Frances Densmore

20th

IN BEAUTY MAY I WALK

In beauty may I walk;
All day long may I walk;
Through the returning seasons may I walk.

Beautifully will I possess again
Beautifully birds
Beautifully butterflies . . .

On the trail marked with pollen may I walk;
With grasshoppers about my feet may I walk;
With dew around my feet may I walk.

With beauty before me may I walk
With beauty behind me may I walk
With beauty above me may I walk
With beauty all around me,
may I walk.

In old age, wandering on a trail of beauty, lively;
In old age, wandering on a trail of beauty, living again . . .
It is finished in beauty.
It is finished in beauty.

Diné (Navajo) night chant,
translated by Jerome K. Rothenberg

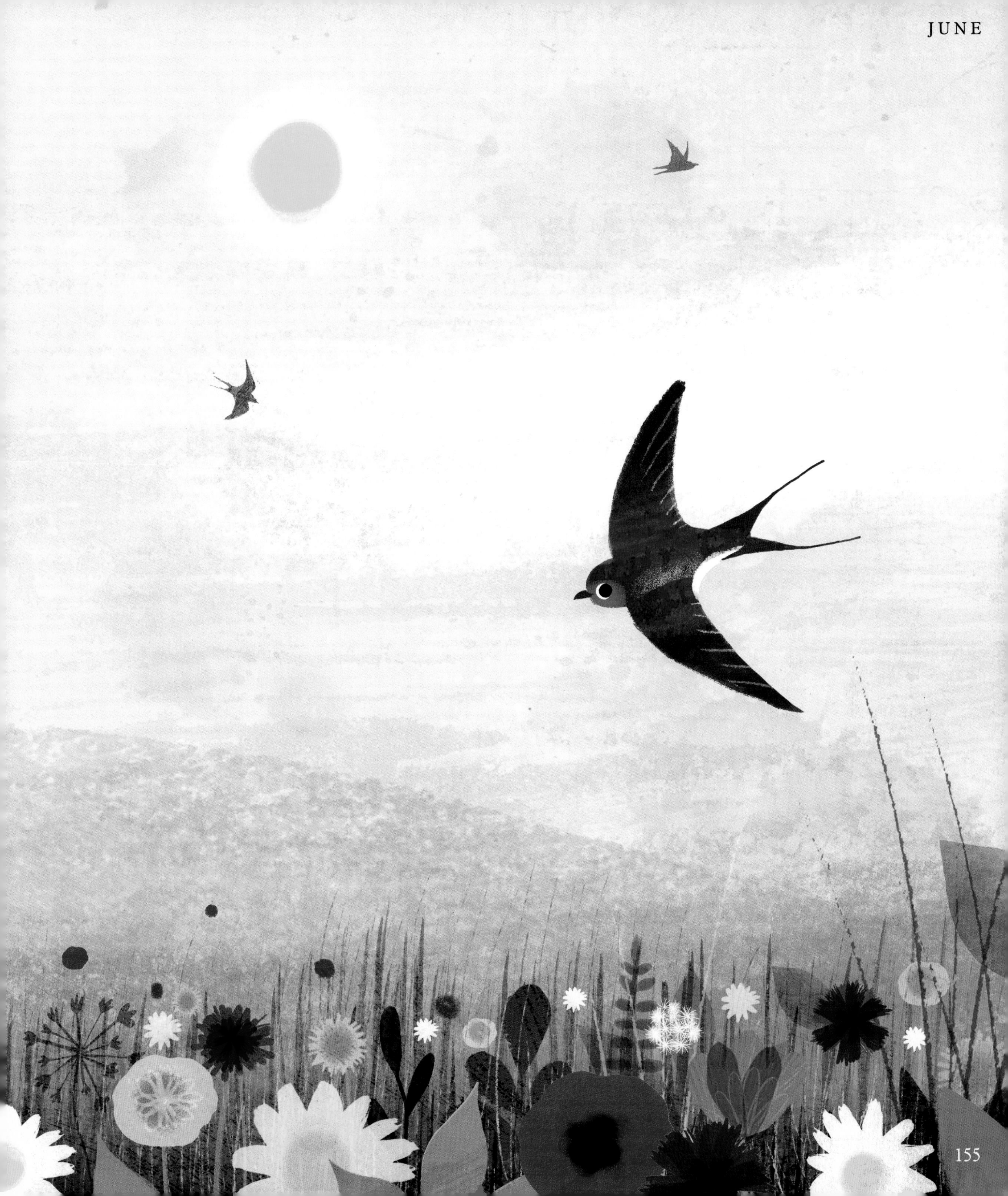

21ˢᵗ

PUDDLE

The moon, the stars, the clouds, a plane
And all that my sky can contain
Reflected in a pool of rain.

This is the eye that follows the sky.

A sheet lain on the bare terrain
That's picture-smooth and mirror-plain
Like looking through a window-pane.

This is the mouth that swallows the sky.

Brilliant echo, bright refrain
Each tiny detail you retain
Write it down and tell it again.

This is the hand that borrows the sky.

Reflected in a pool of rain
My sky with what it can contain:
A bird, the sun, a plane again.

Nick Toczek

22ⁿᵈ

THE SUN HAS
LONG BEEN SET

The sun has long been set,
The stars are out by twos and threes,
The little birds are piping yet
Among the bushes and trees;
There's a cuckoo, and one or two thrushes,
And a far-off wind that rushes,
And a sound of water that gushes,
And the cuckoo's sovereign cry
Fills all the hollow of the sky.
Who would go parading
In London, and masquerading
On such a night of June
With that beautiful soft half-moon,
And all these innocent blisses?
On such a night as this is!

William Wordsworth

23rd

THE POND

Cold, wet leaves
Floating on moss-colored water
And the croaking of frogs—
Cracked bell-notes in the twilight.

Amy Lowell

24th

ONE, TWO, THREE, FOUR, FIVE

One, two, three, four, five,
Once I caught a fish alive.
Six, seven, eight, nine, ten,
Then I let it go again.
Why did you let it go?
Because it bit my finger so.
Which finger did it bite?
This little finger on the right.

Anonymous

25th

WHERE GO THE BOATS

Dark brown is the river,
Golden is the sand.
It flows along forever,
With trees on either hand.

Green leaves a-floating,
Castles of the foam,
Boats of mine a-boating—
Where will all come home?

On goes the river
And out past the mill,
Away down the valley,
Away down the hill.

Away down the river,
A hundred miles or more,
Other little children
Shall bring my boats ashore.

Robert Louis Stevenson

26th

LEAF BOATS

Rain
down
the
drain
    is a waterfall.

A leaf sails along.
A twig starts to float.

I watch
as they bob
and they bounce
down
the
drain.

I see
the rain
drowning
each tiny, wet boat.

Myra Cohn Livingston

27th

WHAT DO YOU SUPPOSE?

What do you suppose?
A bee sat on my nose.
Then what do you think?
He gave me a wink
And said, "I beg your pardon,
I thought you were the garden."

Anonymous

28th

INSECT

Inspect
an insect
and you'll see
how perfect
it can be.

Listen,
and hear
the tiny song
it sings,

as bits of rainbow
glisten
on its wings.

Tony Mitton

29th

ALL DAY LONG

All day long having
buried himself
in the peonies,
the golden bee's
belly is swollen.

Kanoko Okamoto,
translated by Kenneth Rexroth
and Ikuko Atsumi

30th

A HOT DAY

Cottonwool clouds loiter.
A lawnmower, very far,
Birrs. Then a bee comes
To a crimson rose and softly,
Deftly and fatly crams
A velvet body in.

A tree, June-lazy, makes
A tent of dim green light.
Sunlight weaves in the leaves,
Honey-light laced with leaf-light,
Green interleaved with gold.
Sunlight gathers its rays
In sheaves, which the wind unweaves
And then reweaves — the wind
That puffs a smell of grass
Through the heat-heavy, trembling
Summer pool of air.

A. S. J. Tessimond

JULY

1ST

SHADOWS

Stand with your back
to the shining sun;
watch your shadow
dance and run.

Stand and face
the shining sun;
look ahead—
your shadow's gone!

Judith Nicholls

2nd

The falling flower
I saw drift back to the branch
Was a butterfly.

*Arakida Moritake,
translator unknown*

3rd

SLOWLY

Slowly the tide creeps up the sand,
Slowly the shadows cross the land.
Slowly the cart-horse pulls his mile,
Slowly the old man mounts the stile.

Slowly the hands move round the clock,
Slowly the dew dries on the dock.
Slow is the snail—but slowest of all
The green moss spreads on the old brick wall.

James Reeves

4th
SEA CLIFF

Wave on wave
and green on rock
and white between
the splash and black
the crash and hiss
of the feathery fall,
the snap and shock
of the water wall
and the wall of rock:
after —
after the ebb-flow,
wet rock,
high —
high over the slapping green,
water sliding away
and the rock abiding,
new rock riding
out of the spray.

A. J. M. Smith

5th

IF YOU EVER

If you ever ever ever ever ever
   If you ever ever ever meet a whale
You must never never never never never
   You must never never never touch its tail;
For if you ever ever ever ever ever
   If you ever ever ever touch its tail,
You will never never never never never
   You will never never meet another whale.

Anonymous

6th

She sells sea shells on the seashore.
The shells she sells are sea shells I'm sure.
If she sells sea shells on the seashore,
Where are the seashore shells she sells?

Anonymous

7th

INSIDE A SHELL

Inside a shell
There is the whisper of a wave.
Inside a feather
There is the breath of a breeze.
Inside an ember
There is the memory of a flame.
Inside a rock
There is the murmur of a mountain.
Inside a well
There is the echo of a wish.
Inside a seed
There is the promise of a flower.

John Foster

8th

FIVE LITTLE PEAS

Five little peas in a pea-pod pressed,
One grew, two grew and so did all the rest.
They grew and grew and did not stop,
Until one day the pod went POP!

Anonymous

9th

THE BACK STEP

Every day at sunset
We watch the cows go by.
We always like to be there,
My grandmother and I.

They always go to water
Along the same old track,
But some must have a wander
And some go quickly back.

There's Mabel, Maude and Judy,
Mitzi who's always late
And Betsy Anne, who's rubbing
Her flanks against the gate.

Not for them the drabness
Of car or bike or train.
For them it's warming sunshine
And clear, refreshing rain.

It's giving milk each morning
And dozing in the grass.
It's never thinking over
How each new day will pass.

And we can share a little
In all this peace around,
Sitting on the back step
Scratching on the ground.

And so we dream together
And watch the cows go by,
While shelling peas and chatting—
My grandmother and I.

Lee Knowles

10th

MOTH

A moth is a butterfly's dark twin
dressed in drab wings.
She isn't scary.
Think of her as a different thing—
a plain-clothes fairy.

She loves the electric light
that shines through the window,
just like guess-who
when she's flying in from the garden.
Yes, you!

The moth doesn't bite
or scratch or sting.
She can only hurt herself—
flying too close to the light,
burning her wings.

Carol Ann Duffy

171

11th

WHAT HAPPENS
TO THE COLORS?

What happens to the colors
when night replaces day?
What turns the wrens to ravens,
the trees to shades of gray?

Who paints away the garden
when the sky's a sea of ink?
Who robs the sleeping flowers
of their purple and their pink?

What makes the midnight clover
quiver black upon the lawn?
What happens to the colors?
What brings them back at dawn?

Jack Prelutsky

12th
THE MOON AT
KNOWLE HILL

The moon was married last night
and nobody saw
dressed up in her ghostly dress
for the summer ball.

The stars shimmied in the sky
and danced a whirligig;
the moon vowed to be true
and lit up the corn-rigs.

She kissed the dark lips of the sky
above the summer house,
she in her pale white dress
swooned across the vast sky.

The moon was married last night,
the beautiful belle of the ball,
and nobody saw her at all
except a small girl in a navy dress

who witnessed it all.

Jackie Kay

13th
THE SONG OF HAU,
THE RED FOX

On the stone ridge east I go.
On the white road I, red fox, crouching go.
I, red fox, whistle on the road of stars.

Wintu song, translated by Jeremiah Curtin

14th

FIRST FOX

A big fox stands in the spring grass,
Glossy in the sun, chestnut bright,
Plumb centre of the open meadow, a leaf
From a picture book.

Forepaws delicately nervous,
Thick brush on the grass
He rakes the air for the scent
Of the train rushing by.

My first fox,
Wiped from my eye,
In a moment of train-time.

Pamela Gillilan

15th

The blue water in
The Mountain canyon
The grizzly bear on the mountain
Is digging

*Southern Paiute song,
translated by John Wesley Powell*

16th

A DRAGONFLY

When the heat of the summer
Made drowsy the land,
A dragonfly came
And sat on my hand,
With its blue jointed body,
And wings like spun glass,
It lit on my fingers
As though they were grass.

Eleanor Farjeon

17th

RIVER

boat-carrier
bank-lapper
home-provider
tree-reflector
leaf-catcher
field-wanderer
stone-smoother
fast-mover
gentle-stroller
sun-sparkler
sea-seeker

June Crebbin

18th

A clear waterfall;
Into the ripples
Fall green pine-needles.

Matsuo Bashō,
translated by R. H. Blyth

19th

I WISH . . .

I wish I was
a dragonfly
hallelujah
in sungleam.

Anonymous

20th

IT WAS / SO HOT . . .

it was
so hot
that
the flowers
had
to use
their
colours
as fans.

Malcolm de Chazal

21st

COLOURING IN

And staying inside the lines
Is fine, but . . .
I like it when stuff leaks —
When the blue bird and the blue sky
Are just one blur of blue blue flying,
And the feeling of the feathers in the air
And the wind along the blade of wing
Is a long gash of smudgy colour.
I like it when the flowers and the sunshine
Puddle red and yellow into orange,
The way the hot sun on my back
Lulls me — muddles me — sleepy
In the scented garden,
Makes me part of the picture . . .
Part of the place.

Jan Dean

22nd

Where the bee sucks, there suck I:
In a cowslip's bell I lie:
There I couch when owls do cry.
On the bat's back I do fly
After summer merrily.
Merrily, merrily shall I live now
Under the blossom that hangs on the bough.

William Shakespeare, The Tempest

23rd

LAVENDER'S BLUE

Lavender's blue, dilly, dilly,
   Lavender's green,
When I am king, dilly, dilly,
   You shall be queen.

Call up your men, dilly, dilly,
   Set them to work,
Some to the plough, dilly, dilly,
   Some to the cart.

Some to make hay, dilly, dilly,
   Some to thresh corn,
Whilst you and I, dilly, dilly,
   Keep ourselves warm.

Anonymous

24th

THE STORM

We wake to hear the storm come down,
    Sudden on roof and pane;
The thunder's loud and the hasty wind
    Hurries the beating rain.

The rain slackens, the wind blows gently,
    The gust grows gentle and stills,
And the thunder, like a breaking stick,
    Stumbles about the hills.

The drops still hang on leaf and thorn,
    The downs stand up more green;
The sun comes out again in power
    And the sky is washed and clean.

Edward Shanks

25th

SKY'S DAUGHTER

If you walk into mist a story begins
If you eat snow snowmen appear in your dreams
If you see the moon in a pond you're nearly grown up
Falling in streams brings you good luck
    These are the laws of water, sky's daughter

If you watch a river too long you start to feel old
One cup of water is worth two buckets of gold
If you watch clouds long enough a dragon appears
Icicles don't grow on my grandfather's beard
    These are the laws of water, sky's daughter

If you watch the wild sea you start to grow wise
If you leave a tap running a cactus plant cries
At the centre of whirlpools devils make plans
Goblins hide in watering-cans
    These are the laws of water, sky's daughter

If you stand in puddles it will help you grow tall
If you watch the tides turn you sometimes feel small
Sleeping lakes dream of fish falling through air
Waterfalls are rivers washing their hair
        These are the laws of water, sky's daughter

Matt Black

26th

THISTLES

Thirty thirsty thistles
Thicketed and green
Growing in a grassy swamp
Purple-topped and lean
Prickily and thistley
Topped by tufts of thorns
Green mean little leaves on them
And tiny purple horns
Briary and brambley
A spikey, spiney bunch of them.
A troop of bright-red birds came by
And had a lovely lunch of them.

Karla Kuskin

27th

COW

The Cow comes home swinging
Her udder and singing:

"The dirt O the dirt
It does me no hurt.

And a good splash of muck
Is a blessing of luck.

O I splosh through the mud
But the breath of my cud

Is sweeter than silk.
O I splush through manure

But my heart stays pure
As a pitcher of milk."

Ted Hughes

28th

THE PASTURE

I'm going out to clean the pasture spring;
I'll only stop to rake the leaves away
(And wait to watch the water clear, I may):
I shan't be gone long. — You come too.

I'm going out to fetch the little calf
That's standing by the mother. It's so young
It totters when she licks it with her tongue.
I shan't be gone long. — You come too.

Robert Frost

29th

LITTLEMOUSE

Light of day going,
Harvest moon glowing,
People beginning to snore,
Tawny owl calling,
Dead of night falling,
Littlemouse opening her door.

Scrabbling and tripping,
Sliding and slipping,
Over the ruts of the plough,
Under the field gate,
Mustn't arrive late,
Littlemouse hurrying now.

Into a clearing,
All the birds cheering,
Woodpecker blowing a horn,
Nightingale fluting,
Blackbird toot-tooting,
Littlemouse dancing till dawn.

Soon comes the morning,
No time for yawning,
Home again Littlemouse creeps,
Over the furrow,
Back to her burrow,
Into bed. Littlemouse sleeps.

Richard Edwards

30th

THE FALLING STAR

I saw a star slide down the sky,
Blinding the north as it went by,
Too lovely to be bought or sold,
Too burning and too quick to hold,
Good only to make wishes on
And then forever to be gone.

Sara Teasdale

31st

SOME ONE

Some one came knocking
    At my wee, small door;
Some one came knocking,
    I'm sure — sure — sure;
I listened, I opened,
    I looked to left and right,
But nought there was a-stirring
    In the still dark night;
Only the busy beetle
    Tap-tapping in the wall,
Only from the forest
    The screech-owl's call,
Only the cricket whistling
    While the dewdrops fall,
So I know not who came knocking,
    At all, at all, at all.

Walter de la Mare

AUGUST

1st   **IF ALL THE SEAS WERE ONE SEA**   *Anonymous*

2nd   **UNTIL I SAW THE SEA**   *Lilian Moore*

3rd   **THE LAKE ISLE OF INNISFREE**   *William Butler Yeats*

4th   **SQUISHY WORDS (TO BE SAID WHEN WET)**   *Alastair Reid*

5th   **AT THE SEASIDE**   *Robert Louis Stevenson*

6th   **SEA SHELL**   *Amy Lowell*

7th   **THE SHELL**   *John Foster*

8th   **DAYS**   *Brian Moses*

9th   **AUGUST HEAT**   *Anonymous*

10th   **THE MOCKINGBIRD'S SONG**   *Tigua song, translated by John Comfort Fillmore*

11th   **I AM THE RAIN**   *Grace Nichols*

12th   **LITTLE FISH**   *D. H. Lawrence*

13th   **THERE WAS AN OLD MAN IN A TREE**   *Edward Lear*

14th   **EVERY TIME I CLIMB A TREE**   *David McCord*

15th   **SEAL**   *William Jay Smith*

1st

IF ALL THE SEAS
WERE ONE SEA

If all the seas were one sea,
What a great sea that would be!
If all the trees were one tree,
What a great tree that would be!
And if all the axes were one axe,
What a great axe that would be!
And if all the men were one man,
What a great man that would be!
And if the great man took the great axe
And cut down the great tree,
And let it fall into the great sea,
What a splish-splash that would be!

Anonymous

2nd

UNTIL I SAW THE SEA

Until I saw the sea
I did not know
that wind
could wrinkle water so.

I never knew
that sun
could splinter a whole sea of blue.

Nor
did I know before
a sea breathes in and out
upon a shore.

Lilian Moore

3rd

THE LAKE ISLE OF INNISFREE

I will arise and go now, and go to Innisfree,
And a small cabin build there, of clay and wattles made:
Nine bean rows will I have there, a hive for the honey bee,
And live alone in the bee-loud glade.

And I shall have some peace there, for peace comes dropping slow,
Dropping from the veils of the morning to where the cricket sings;
There midnight's all a glimmer, and noon a purple glow,
And evening full of the linnet's wings.

I will arise and go now, for always night and day
I hear lake water lapping with low sounds by the shore;
While I stand on the roadway, or on the pavements grey,
I hear it in the deep heart's core.

William Butler Yeats

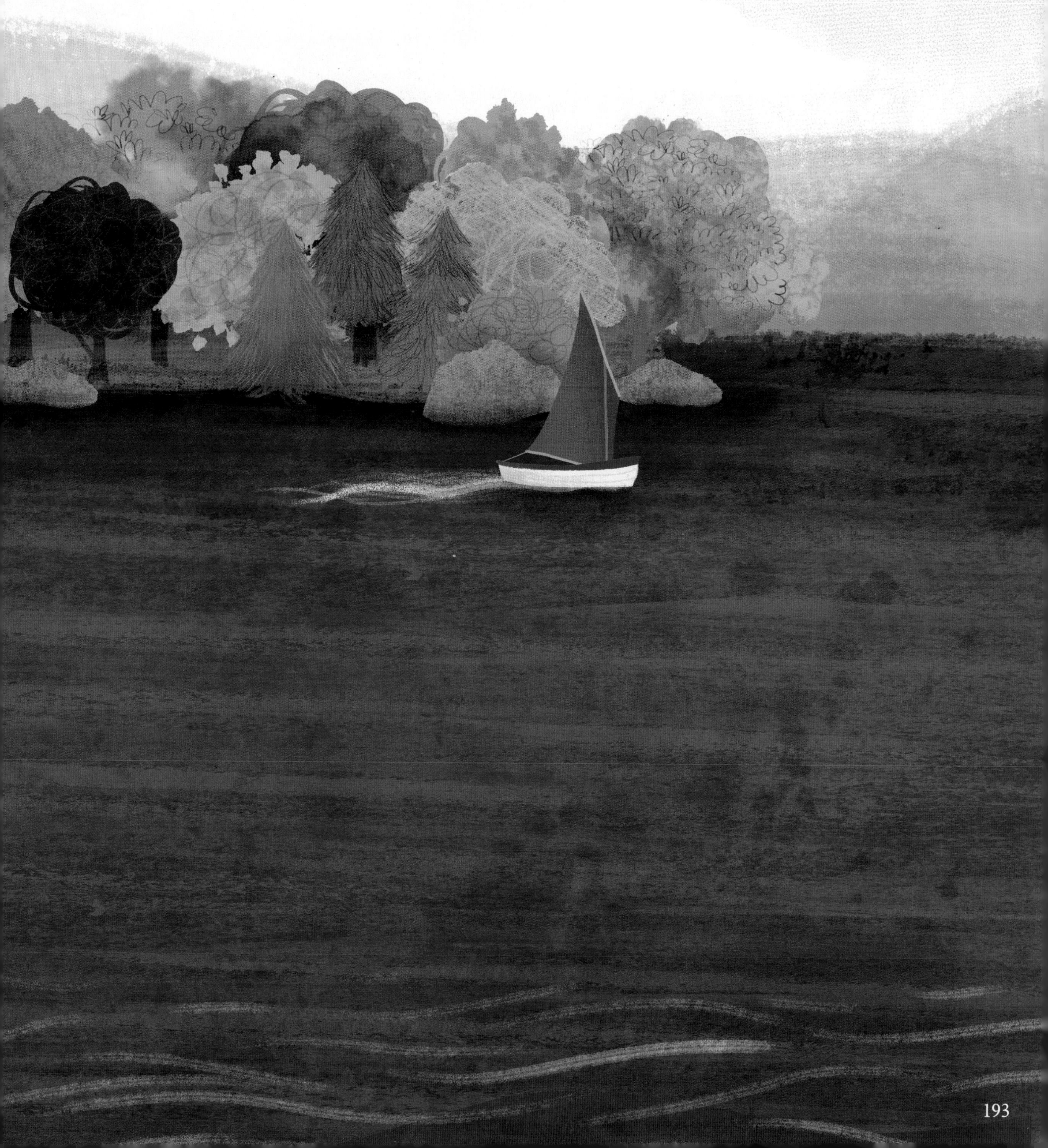

4th

SQUISHY WORDS
(TO BE SAID WHEN WET)

SQUIFF
SQUIDGE
SQUAMOUS
SQUINNY
SQUELCH
SQUASH
SQUEEGEE
SQUIRT
SQUAB

Alastair Reid

5th

AT THE SEASIDE

When I was down beside the sea
A wooden spade they gave to me
To dig the sandy shore.
My holes were empty like a cup,
In every hole the sea came up,
Till it could come no more.

Robert Louis Stevenson

6th

SEA SHELL

Sea Shell, Sea Shell,
Sing me a song, O Please!
A song of ships, and sailor men,
And parrots, and tropical trees,

Of islands lost in the Spanish Main
Which no man ever may find again,
Of fishes and corals under the waves,
And sea horses stabled in great green caves.

Sea Shell, Sea Shell,
Sing of the things you know so well.

Amy Lowell

7th

THE SHELL

On the shelf in my bedroom stands a shell.
If I hold it close, I can smell
The salty sea.
I can hear the slap
Of the waves as they lap
The sandy shore.
I can feel once more
The tickling tide
As it gently flows between my toes.

John Foster

8th

DAYS

Days fly by on holidays,
they escape like birds
released from cages.
What a shame you can't buy
tokens of time, save them up
and lengthen the good days,
or maybe you could tear out time
from days that drag, then pay it back
on holidays, wild days,
days you wish would last forever.
You could wear these days with pride,
fasten them like poppies to your coat,
or keep them in a tin, like sweets,
a confection of days
to be held on the tongue
and tasted, now and then.

Brian Moses

9th

AUGUST HEAT

In August, when the days are hot,
I like to find a shady spot,
And hardly move a single bit—
And sit—
    And sit—
      And sit—
        And sit!

Anonymous

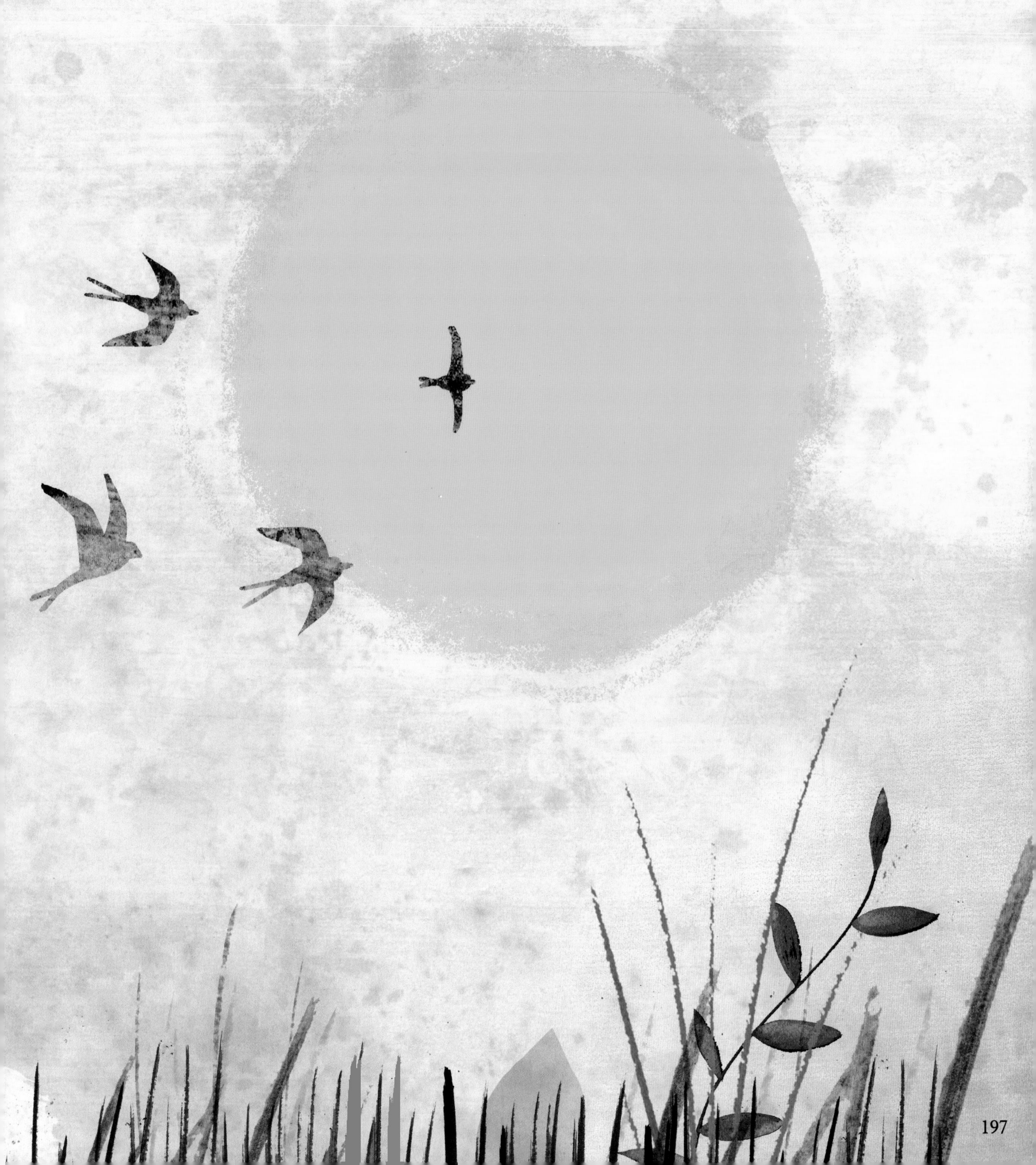

10th

THE MOCKINGBIRD'S SONG

Rain, people, rain!
The rain is all around us.
It is going to come pouring down,
And the summer will be fair to see,
The mockingbird has said so.

Tigua song, translated by John Comfort Fillmore

11th

I AM THE RAIN

I am the rain
I like to play games
like sometimes
    I pretend
I'm going
    to fall
Man that's the time
I don't come at all

Like sometimes
I get these laughing stitches
up my sides
    rushing people in
and out
    with the clothesline
I just love drip
    dropping
down collars
    and spines
Maybe it's a shame
but it's the only way
I get some fame

Grace Nichols

12th

LITTLE FISH

The tiny fish enjoy themselves
in the sea.
Quick little splinters of life,
their little lives are fun to them
in the sea.

D. H. Lawrence

13th

THERE WAS AN OLD MAN IN A TREE

There was an Old Man in a tree,
Who was horribly bored by a bee.
When they said, "Does it buzz?"
He replied, "Yes, it does!
It's a regular brute of a bee!"

Edward Lear

14th

EVERY TIME I CLIMB A TREE

Every time I climb a tree
Every time I climb a tree
Every time I climb a tree
I scrape a leg
Or skin a knee
And every time I climb a tree
I find some ants
Or dodge a bee
And get the ants
All over me

And every time I climb a tree
Where have you been?
They say to me
But don't they know that I am free
Every time I climb a tree?
I like it best
To spot a nest
That has an egg
Or maybe three

And then I skin
The other leg
But every time I climb a tree
I see a lot of things to see
Swallows, rooftops and TV
And all the fields and farms there be
Every time I climb a tree
Though climbing may be good for ants
It isn't awfully good for pants
But still it's pretty good for me
Every time I climb a tree

David McCord

15th

SEAL

See how he dives
From the rocks with a zoom!
See how he darts
Through his watery room
Past crabs and eels
And green seaweed,
Past fluffs of sandy
Minnow feed!
See how he swims
With a swerve and a twist,
A flip of the flipper,
A flick of the wrist!
Quicksilver-quick,
Softer than spray,
Down he plunges
And sweeps away;
Before you can think,
Before you can utter
Words like "Dill pickle"
Or "Apple butter,"
Back up he swims
Past stingray and shark,
Out with a zoom,
A whoop, a bark;
Before you can say
Whatever you wish,
He plops at your side
With a mouthful of fish!

William Jay Smith

16th

THE PIKE

In the brown water,
Thick and silver-sheened in the sunshine,
Liquid and cool in the shade of the reeds,
A pike dozed.
Lost among the shadows of stems
He lay unnoticed.
Suddenly he flicked his tail,
And a green-and-copper brightness
Ran under the water.

Out from under the reeds
Came the olive-green light,
And orange flashed up
Through the sun-thickened water.
So the fish passed across the pool,
Green and copper,
A darkness and a gleam,
And the blurred reflections of the willows
    on the opposite bank
Received it.

Amy Lowell

17th

BROWN-RIVER
BROWN-RIVER

Brown-River
Brown-River
Why do you run
You must be trying
To catch-up with someone?

O I'm on my way
To catch-up with the sea
But however fast I run
There's always more of me
Always more of me.

Grace Nichols

18th

ROW, ROW, ROW
YOUR BOAT

Row, row, row your boat
Gently down the stream.
Merrily, merrily, merrily, merrily,
Life is but a dream.

Anonymous

19th

THE LAST ROSE
OF SUMMER (EXTRACT)

'Tis the last rose of summer
Left blooming alone;
All her lovely companions
Are faded and gone;
No flower of her kindred,
No rosebud is nigh,
To reflect back her blushes,
To give sigh for sigh.

Thomas Moore

20th

WHAT IS PINK?

What is pink? A rose is pink
By the fountain's brink.
What is red? A poppy's red
In its barley bed.
What is blue? The sky is blue
Where the clouds float through.
What is white? A swan is white
Sailing in the light.
What is yellow? Pears are yellow,
Rich and ripe and mellow.
What is green? The grass is green,
With small flowers between.
What is violet? Clouds are violet
In the summer twilight.
What is orange? Why, an orange,
Just an orange!

Christina Rossetti

21st

THE SECRET SONG

Who saw the petals
    drop from the rose?
I, said the spider,
But nobody knows.

Who saw the sunset
    flash on a bird?
I, said the fish,
But nobody heard.

Who saw the fog
    come over the sea?
I, said the sea pigeon,
Only me.

Who saw the first
    green light of the sun?
I, said the night owl,
The only one.

Who saw the moss
    creep over the stone?
I, said the gray fox,
All alone.

Margaret Wise Brown

22nd

WE HAVE A
LITTLE GARDEN

We have a little garden,
    A garden of our own,
And every day we water there
    The seeds that we have sown.

We love our little garden,
    And tend it with such care,
You will not find a faded leaf
    Or blighted blossom there.

Beatrix Potter

23rd

THE EAGLE

He clasps the crag with crooked hands;
Close to the sun in lonely lands,
Ringed with the azure world, he stands.

The wrinkled sea beneath him crawls;
He watches from his mountain walls,
And like a thunderbolt he falls.

Alfred, Lord Tennyson

24th

HURRICANE

Shut the windows
Bolt the doors
Big rain coming
Climbing up the mountain

Neighbors whisper
Dark clouds gather
Big rain coming
Climbing up the mountain

Gather in the clotheslines
Pull down the blinds
Big wind rising
Coming up the mountain

Branches falling
Raindrops flying
Treetops swaying
People running
Big wind blowing
Hurricane! on the mountain.

Dionne Brand

25th

I WENT UP
THE HIGH HILL

I went up the high hill,
There I saw a climbing goat;
I went down by the running rill,
There I saw a ragged sheep;
I went out to the roaring sea,
There I saw a tossing boat;
I went under the green tree,
There I saw two doves asleep.

Anonymous

26th

IS THE MOON TIRED?

Is the moon tired? She looks so pale
    Within her misty veil;
She scales the sky from east to west,
    And takes no rest.

Before the coming of the night
    The moon shows papery white;
Before the dawning of the day
    She fades away.

Christina Rossetti

27th

On the low-tide beach,
Everything we pick up
Moves.

Fukuda Chiyo-ni,
translated by R. H. Blyth

28th

THE SILVER ROAD

Last night I saw a Silver Road
    Go straight across the Sea;
And quick as I raced along the Shore,
    That quick Road followed me.

It followed me all round the Bay,
    Where small Waves danced in tune;
And at the end of the Silver Road
    There hung a Silver Moon.

A large round Moon on a pale green Sky,
    With a Pathway bright and broad;
Some night I shall bring that Silver Moon
    Across that Silver Road!

Hamish Hendry

29th

MAGGIE AND MILLY
AND MOLLY AND MAY

maggie and milly and molly and may
went down to the beach (to play one day)

and maggie discovered a shell that sang
so sweetly she couldn't remember her troubles, and

milly befriended a stranded star
whose rays five languid fingers were;

and molly was chased by a horrible thing
which raced sideways while blowing bubbles:and

may came home with a smooth round stone
as small as a world and as large as alone.

For whatever we lose (like a you or a me)
it's always ourselves we find in the sea

E. E. Cummings

30th

DOING NOTHING MUCH

I could potter for hours on a lonely beach
Picking pebbles to roll in my hand,
Wondering where will the next wave reach,
Writing my name in the sand.

Near the tumbling weir, where the hawthorn's pink,
I could sit for hours in a trance
Watching the water stream to the brink
And the white foam pound and dance.

Or high on a headland find me,
While a seagull wheels and dips,
Gazing for hours out to sea
At islands and smudges of ships.

Eric Finney

31st

THE BLACK PEBBLE

There went three children down to the shore
    Down to the shore and back;
There was skipping Susan and bright-eyed Sam
    And little scowling Jack.

Susan found a white cockle shell,
    The prettiest ever seen,
And Sam picked up a piece of glass
    Rounded and smooth and green.

But Jack found only a plain black pebble
    That lay by the rolling sea,
And that was all that ever he found;
    So back they went all three.

The cockle shell they put on the table,
    The green glass on the shelf,
But the little black pebble that Jack had found
    He kept it for himself.

James Reeves

SEPTEMBER

1st

TO A RED KITE

Fling
yourself
upon the sky.

Take the string
you need.
Ride high

high
above the park.
Tug and buck
and lark
with the wind.

Touch a cloud,
red kite.
Follow the wild geese
in their flight.

Lilian Moore

2nd

SUMMER GOES

Summer goes, summer goes
Like the sand between my toes
When the waves go out.
That's how summer pulls away,
Leaves me standing here today,
Waiting for the school bus.

Summer brought, summer brought
All the frogs that I have caught,
Frogging at the pond,
Hot dogs, flowers, shells and rocks,
Postcards in my postcard box—
Places far away.

Summer took, summer took
All the lessons in my book,
Blew them far away.
I forgot the things I knew—
Arithmetic and spelling too,
Never thought about them.

Summer's gone, summer's gone—
Fall and winter coming on,
Frosty in the morning.
Here's the school bus right on time.
I'm not really sad that I'm
Going back to school.

Russell Hoban

3rd

FROM A DAKOTA WHEAT-FIELD

Like liquid gold the wheat-field lies,
    A marvel of yellow and russet and green,
That ripples and runs, that floats and flies,
    With the subtle shadows, the change,
        the sheen,
      That play in the golden hair of a girl—
        A ripple of amber—a flare
    Of light sweeping after—a curl
In the hollows like swirling feet
      Of fairy waltzers, the colors run
      To the western sun
Through the deeps of
        the ripening wheat.

Hamlin Garland

4th

HAYING

From the soft dyke-road, crooked and waggon-worn,
Comes the great load of rustling scented hay,
Slow-drawn with heavy swing and creaky sway
Through the cool freshness of the windless morn.
The oxen, yoked and sturdy, horn to horn,
Sharing the rest and toil of night and day,
Bend head and neck to the long hilly way
By many a season's labour marked and torn.
On the broad sea of dyke the gathering heat
Waves upward from the grass, where road on road
Is swept before the tramping of the teams.
And while the oxen rest beside the sweet
New hay, the loft receives the early load,
With hissing stir, among the dusty beams.

John Frederic Herbin

5th

THE SANDPIPER

At the edge of tide
He stops to wonder,
Races through
The lace of thunder.

On toothpick legs
Swift and brittle,
He runs and pipes
And his voice is little.

But small or not,
He has a notion
To outshout
The Atlantic Ocean.

Frances M. Frost

6th

SEA-FEVER

I must go down to the seas again, to the lonely sea and the sky,
And all I ask is a tall ship and a star to steer her by,
And the wheel's kick and the wind's song and the white sail's shaking,
And a grey mist on the sea's face and a grey dawn breaking.

I must go down to the seas again, for the call of the running tide
Is a wild call and a clear call that may not be denied;
And all I ask is a windy day with the white clouds flying,
And the flung spray and the blown spume, and the seagulls crying.

I must go down to the seas again, to the vagrant gypsy life,
To the gull's way and the whale's way where the wind's like a whetted knife;
And all I ask is a merry yarn from a laughing fellow-rover,
And quiet sleep and a sweet dream when the long trick's over.

John Masefield

7th

MY FATHER GAVE ME SEEDS

My father gave me seeds.
I gave the seeds to the earth.
The earth gave me flowers.
I gave the flowers to the bees.
The bees gave me honey.
I gave the honey to a merchant.
The merchant gave me cloth.
I gave the cloth to a tailor.
The tailor gave me a cloak.
I gave the cloak to a farmer.
The farmer gave me seeds.
I gave the seeds to my father.
My father gave thanks for the seeds.

John Foster

8th

THE MAGIC SEEDS

There was an old woman who sowed a corn seed,
And from it there sprouted a tall yellow weed.
She planted the seeds of the tall yellow flower,
And up sprang a blue one in less than an hour.
The seed of the blue one she sowed in a bed,
And up sprang a tall tree with blossoms of red.
And high in the treetop there sang a white bird,
And his song was the sweetest that ever was heard.
The people they came from far and from near,
The song of the little white bird for to hear.

James Reeves

9th

SPIN ME A WEB, SPIDER

Spin me a web, spider,
Across the windowpane
For I shall never break it
And make you start again.

Cast your net of silver
As soon as it is spun,
And hang it with the morning dew
That glitters in the sun.

It's strung with pearls and diamonds,
The finest ever seen,
Fit for any royal King
Or any royal Queen.

Would you, could you, bring it down
In the dust to lie?
Any day of the week, my dear,
Said the nimble fly.

Charles Causley

10th

HURT NO LIVING THING

Hurt no living thing,
Ladybird nor butterfly,
Nor moth with dusty wing,
Nor cricket chirping cheerily,
Nor grasshopper, so light of leap,
Nor dancing gnat,
Nor beetle fat,
Nor harmless worms that creep.

Christina Rossetti

11th

DEW ON A SPIDER'S WEB

Dew on a spider's web is a wonderful sight,
Early morning finds what has been created at night,
Lovely designs spun so nice,
Without a pattern of device,
Looking at a mat of lace,
Shows how long it takes to place.

Dorothy Snow

12th

FOREST END

Since they left the house
the trees moved in;
the oak and ash made a home.
Where the chimney stood
is a jagged pine,
and the roof has almost gone.

Since they left the house
the birds moved in;
you can hear the thrush's song.
The house awakes
to the squawk of rooks,
and sleeps when the owl has flown.

Since they left the house
the winds moved in;
the windows wail and groan.
A few stairs creak
to a clouded sky,
then the house is left, alone.

Judith Nicholls

13th

THE FERNS

High, high in the branches
the seawinds plunge and roar.
A storm is moving westward,
but here on the forest floor
the ferns have captured stillness.
A green sea growth they are.

The ferns lie underwater
in a light of the forest's green.
Their motion is like stillness,
as if water shifts between
and a great storm quivers
through fathoms of green.

Gene Baro

14th

THE DESERTED HOUSE

There's no smoke in the chimney,
    And the rain beats on the floor;
There's no glass in the window,
    There's no wood in the door;
The heather grows behind the house,
    And the sand lies before.

No hand hath trained the ivy,
    The walls are grey and bare;
The boats upon the sea sail by,
    Nor ever tarry there.
No beast of the field comes nigh,
    Nor any bird of the air.

Mary Coleridge

15th

PLUM

Don't be so glum,
plum.

Don't feel beaten.

You were made
to be eaten.

But don't you know
that deep within,
beneath your juicy flesh
and flimsy skin,

you bear a mystery,
you hold a key,

you have the making of
a whole new tree.

Tony Mitton

16th

I HAD A LITTLE NUT TREE

I had a little nut tree, and nothing would it bear
But a silver nutmeg and a golden pear.
The King of Spain's daughter came to visit me
And all for the sake of my little nut tree.
I skipped over water, I danced over sea
But all the birds in the air couldn't catch me.

Anonymous

231

17th

MAGPIES

Along the road the magpies walk
with hands in pockets, left and right.
They tilt their heads, and stroll and talk.
In their well-fitted black and white

they look like certain gentlemen
who seem most nonchalant and wise
until their meal is served — and then
what clashing beaks, what greedy eyes!

But not one man that I have heard
throws back his head in such a song
of grace and praise — no man nor bird.
Their greed is brief; their joy is long.
For each is born with such a throat
as thanks his God with every note.

Judith Wright

18th

SEVEN FOR A SECRET

Seven black birds in a tree,
Count them and see what they be.
One for sorrow
Two for joy
Three for a girl
Four for a boy;
Five for silver
Six for gold
Seven for a secret
That's never been told.

Anonymous

19th

TREE SONG

City of whispers,
symphony of sighs,
intricate embroidery
sampling the skies.

Machinery of nature,
factory of air,
delirious dancer
dishevelling her hair.

Tony Mitton

20th

ACORN HAIKU

Just a green olive
In its own little egg-cup:
It can feed the sky.

Kit Wright

21st

WINDSONG

I am the seed
that grew the tree
that gave the wood
to make the page
to fill the book
with poetry.

Judith Nicholls

22nd

AUGURIES OF INNOCENCE (EXTRACT)

To see a World in a Grain of Sand
And a Heaven in a Wild Flower,
Hold Infinity in the palm of your hand
And Eternity in an hour.

William Blake

23rd

THE MORNS ARE MEEKER
THAN THEY WERE

The morns are meeker than they were,
  The nuts are getting brown;
The berry's cheek is plumper,
  The rose is out of town.

The maple wears a gayer scarf,
  The field a scarlet gown.
Lest I should be old-fashioned,
  I'll put a trinket on.

Emily Dickinson

24th

NOISY, NOISY

It's noisy, noisy overhead,
the birds are winging south,
and every bird is opening
a noisy, noisy mouth.

They fill the air with loud complaint,
they honk and quack and squawk—
they do not feel like flying,
but it's much too far to walk.

Jack Prelutsky

25th

THE SWALLOWS

Nine swallows sat on a telephone wire:
"Teeter, teeter," and then they were still,
all facing one way, with the sun like a fire
along their blue shoulders, and hot on each bill.
But they sat there so quietly, all of the nine,
that I almost forgot they were swallows at all.
They seemed more like clothespins left out on the line
when the wash is just dried, and the first raindrops fall.

Elizabeth Coatsworth

26th

WARNING TO A PERSON SITTING UNDER AN APPLE TREE IN AN AUTUMN GARDEN ON A SUNNY AFTERNOON WITH THEIR NOSE STUCK IN A GOOD BOOK

Directly up above you hanging by a thread
An apple's getting ready to thump you on the head.

June Crebbin

27th

IF I WERE AN APPLE

If I were an apple
And grew upon a tree,
I think I'd fall down
On a good boy like me.
I wouldn't stay there
Giving nobody joy;
I'd fall down at once
And say, "Eat me, my boy."

Anonymous

28th

POEMOLOGY

an apple a day
is 365 apples

a poem a day
is 365 poems
most years

any doctor will tell you
it is easier to eat an apple
than to make a poem

it is also easier
to eat a poem
than to make an apple
but only
just.

      but here
is what you do
to keep the doctor
out of it:

      publish a poem
on your appletree

have an apple
in your next book

Anselm Hollo

29th

APPLES

A cold apple from the dish.
Crunch through its green.
Juice runs sweetly and sourly
in my mouth and down my chin.
Fingers grow sticky, I lick them clean.

John Siddique

30th

NEW SIGHTS

I like to see a thing I know
Has not been seen before,
That's why I cut my apple through
To look into the core.

It's nice to think, though many an eye
Has seen the ruddy skin,
Mine is the very first to spy
The five brown pips within.

Anonymous

OCTOBER

1st

THE LEAVES ARE GREEN

The leaves are green
The nuts are brown,
They hang so high
They will not come down.

Leave them alone
Till frosty weather,
Then they will all
Come down together.

Anonymous

2nd

Under the greenwood tree
Who loves to lie with me,
And turn his merry note
Unto the sweet bird's throat,
Come hither, come hither, come hither!
Here shall he see
No enemy
But winter and rough weather.

William Shakespeare, As You Like It

3rd

THE SQUIRREL

Whisky, frisky,
Hippity hop,
Up he goes
To the treetop!

Whirly, twirly,
Round and round,
Down he scampers
To the ground.

Furly, curly,
What a tail!
Tall as a feather
Broad as a sail!

Where's his supper?
In the shell,
Snappity, crackity,
Out it fell!

Anonymous

4th

HOG IN A WOOD

Big black hog in a wood
On a truffle hunt.
Head stuck deep in the earth —
Grunt, snort, grunt.

    Oh a hog's in heaven when his tongue
    Is wrapped around a truffle.
    His tail uncurls and his hog heart
    Performs a soft-shoe shuffle.

Big black hog in a wood
Chewing muddy truffles.
Great snout nosing them out —
Sniff, snuff, snuffles.

Adrian Mitchell

5th

CONKERS

When chestnuts are hanging
Above the school yard,
They are little green sea-mines
Spiky and hard.

But when they fall bursting
And all the boys race,
Each shines like a jewel
In a satin case.

Clive Sansom

6th

The farmer flings the fruitful seed
Afar upon the furrowed field.

Anonymous

7th

THE SCARECROW

The scarecrow stands
With hanging hands,
Beside the farmer's stile.
He scares the jay and crow away
With just a painted smile.

Anonymous

8th

CLICHÉ

They came between dusk blue
and the watery moon's rising,
arrows of geese
that made the sky a river
flecked with froth.

Their calling silvered the air,
reflected in glass and puddles,
made twilight a cliché.

But one small boy
who knew geese only from a picture book
watched,
gasped,
wondered.

Alison Chisholm

9th

WIND

Now has the wind a sound
Made out of rain;
A misty, broken secretness,
That drenches road and pane.
It drips and drips; a hush
Falls on the town;
Like golden clods an old tree shakes
Its apples down.

Lizette Woodworth Reese

10th

IT'S ONLY THE STORM

"What's that creature that rattles the roof?"
"Hush, it's only the storm."

"What's blowing the tiles and branches off?"
"Hush, it's only the storm."

"What's riding the sky like a wild white horse,
Flashing its teeth and stamping its hooves?"

"Hush, my dear, it's only the storm,
Racing the darkness till it catches the dawn.
Hush, my dear, it's only the storm.
When you wake in the morning, it will be gone."

David Greygoose

11th

LIMPET

When big surf slams
His tower so hard
The Lighthouse-keeper's
Teeth are jarred

The Limpet laughs
Beneath her hat:
"There's nothing I love
So much as that!

"Huge seas of shock
That roar to knock me
Off my rocker
Rock me, rock me."

Ted Hughes

12th

THE HAWK

Afternoon,
with just enough of a breeze
    for him to ride it
lazily, a hawk
sails still-winged
up the slope of a stubble-covered hill,
so low
he nearly
touches his shadow

Robert Sund

13th

THE MOUNTAIN PEAK

On the peak of the mountain
The eagle is dancing,
The tempest is roaring

*Southern Paiute song,
translated by John Wesley Powell*

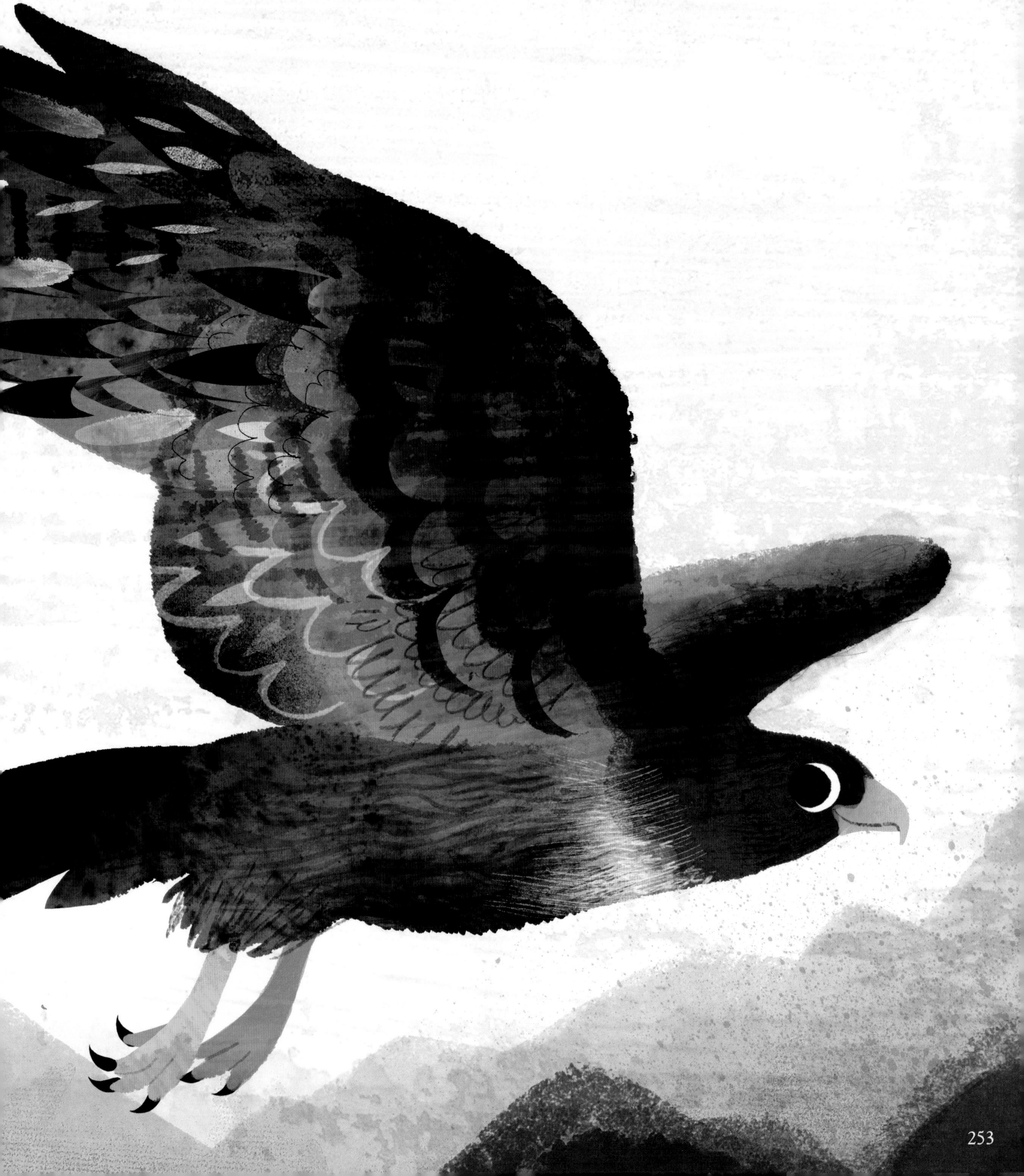

14th

RAIN POEM

The rain was like a little mouse,
Quiet, small, and gray,
It pattered all around the house
And then it went away.
It did not come, I understand,
Indoors at all, until,
It found an open window and
Left tracks across the sill.

Elizabeth Coatsworth

15th

RAIN SIZES

Rain comes in various sizes.
Some rain is as small as a mist.
It tickles your face with surprises,
And tingles as if you'd been kissed.

Some rain is the size of a sprinkle
And doesn't put out all the sun.
You can see the drops sparkle and twinkle,
And a rainbow comes out when it's done.

Some rain is as big as a nickel
And comes with a crash and a hiss.
It comes down too heavy to tickle.
It's more like a splash than a kiss.

When it rains the right size and you're wrapped in
Your rainclothes, it's fun out of doors.
But run home before you get trapped in
The big rain that rattles and roars.

John Ciardi

16th

First winter rain:
The monkey also seems
To want a small straw cloak.

Matsuo Bashō,
translated by R. H. Blyth

17th

THE RAIN

Rain on the green grass,
   And rain on the tree,
And rain on the house-top.
   But not upon me!

Anonymous

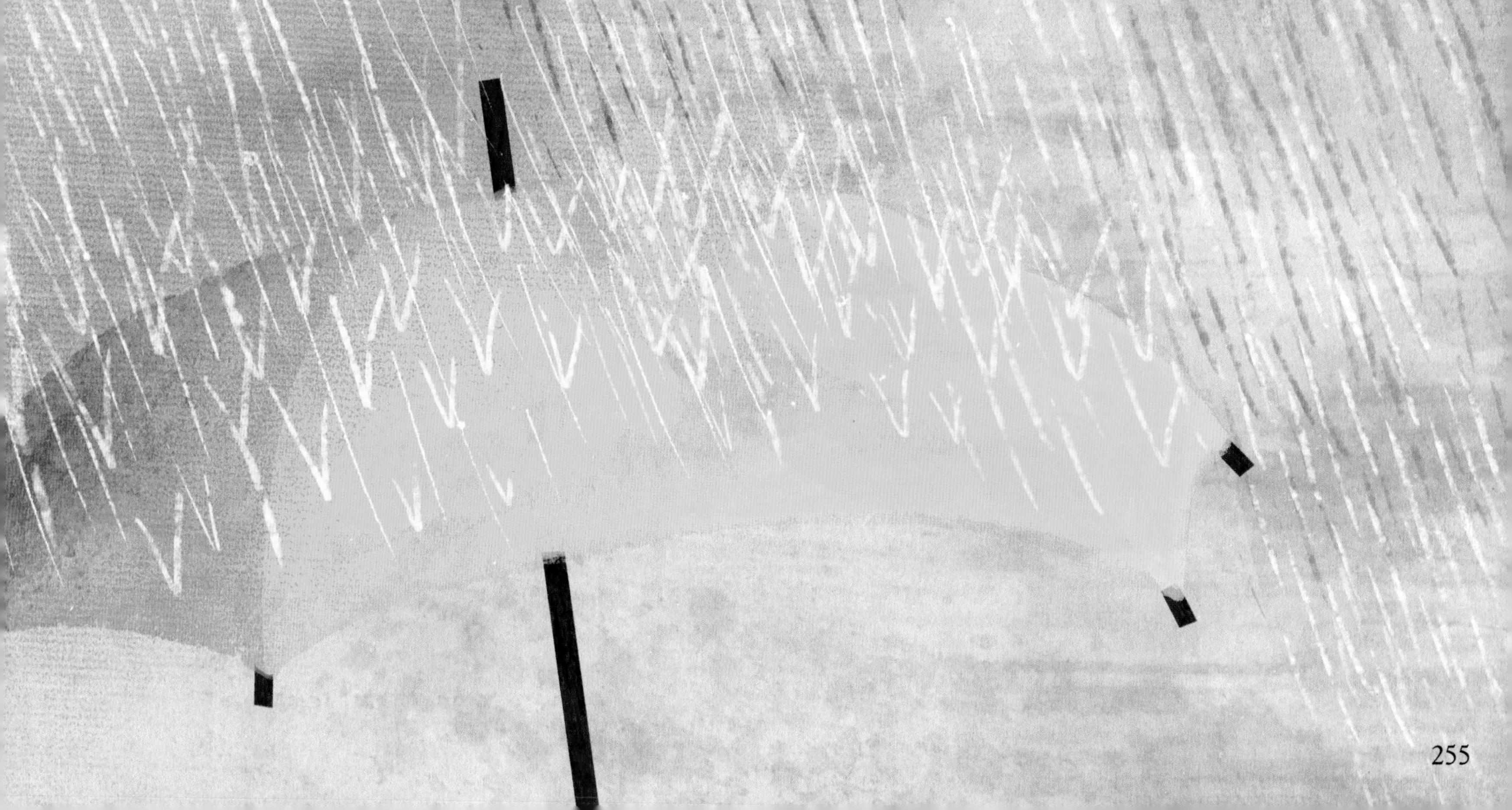

18th

THE ROAD NOT TAKEN

Two roads diverged in a yellow wood,
And sorry I could not travel both
And be one traveler, long I stood
And looked down one as far as I could
To where it bent in the undergrowth;

Then took the other, as just as fair,
And having perhaps the better claim,
Because it was grassy and wanted wear;
Though as for that the passing there
Had worn them really about the same,

And both that morning equally lay
In leaves no step had trodden black.
Oh, I kept the first for another day!
Yet knowing how way leads on to way,
I doubted if I should ever come back.

I shall be telling this with a sigh
Somewhere ages and ages hence:
Two roads diverged in a wood, and I—
I took the one less traveled by,
And that has made all the difference.

Robert Frost

19th

AN AUTUMN GREETING

"Come," said the Wind to the Leaves one day.
"Come over the meadow and we will play.
Put on your dresses of red and gold.
For summer is gone and the days grow cold."

George Cooper

20th

Blowing from the west
Fallen leaves gather
In the east.

*Yosa Buson,
translated by R. H. Blyth*

21st

LEAVES

How silently they tumble down
And come to rest upon the ground
To lay a carpet, rich and rare,
Beneath the trees without a care,
Content to sleep, their work well done,
Colours gleaming in the sun.

At other times, they wildly fly
Until they nearly reach the sky.
Twisting, turning through the air
Till all the trees stand stark and bare.
Exhausted, drop to earth below
To wait, like children, for the snow.

Elsie N. Brady

22nd

THE AUTUMN LEAVES

In autumn
the trees wave in the wind
and the leaves come tumbling
   down,
         down,
               down,
                     down.

Here they come,
hundreds and thousands of leaves
in yellow, red,
   hazel,
         gold
               and
                     chocolate brown.

Wes Magee

23rd

FOG

The fog comes
on little cat feet.
It sits looking
over harbor and city
on silent haunches
and then moves on.

Carl Sandburg

24th

NOTHING MOVES

Out on the cobblestones
trots an old hobble-boned horse
on its stone-clopping hooves.

The smoke's licking up
at the cracks in the bricks
and the cat's meowing round at the roofs.

And a dog's barking up at the darkening clouds —

but aside from the horse
and the smoke
and the cat
and the dog
and the clouds —

nothing moves.

JonArno Lawson

25th

WHERE WOULD YOU BE?

Where would you be on a night like this
With the wind so dark and howling?
Close to the light
Wrapped warm and tight
Or there where the cats are prowling?

Where would you wish you on such a night
When the twisting trees are tossed?
Safe in a chair
In the lamp-lit air
Or out where the moon is lost?

Where would you be when the white waves roar
On the tumbling storm-torn sea?
Tucked inside
Where it's calm and dry
Or searching for stars in the furious sky
Whipped by the whine of the gale's wild cry
Out in the night with me?

Karla Kuskin

26th

LUV SONG

I am in luv wid a hedgehog
I've never felt dis way before
I have luv fe dis hedgehog
An everyday I luv her more an more,
She lives by de shed
Where weeds an roses bed
An I just want de world to know
She makes me glow.

I am in luv wid a hedgehog
She's making me hair stand on edge,
So in luv wid dis hedgehog
An her friends
Who all live in de hedge
She visits me late
An eats off Danny's plate
But Danny's a cool tabby cat
He leaves it at dat.

I am in luv wid a hedgehog,
She's gone away so I must wait
But I do miss my hedgehog
Everytime she goes to hibernate.

Benjamin Zephaniah

27th

MICE

I think mice
Are rather nice.

Their tails are long,
Their faces small,
They haven't any
Chins at all.
Their ears are pink,
Their teeth are white,
They run about
The house at night.
They nibble things
They shouldn't touch
And no one seems
To like them much.

But I think mice
Are nice.

Rose Fyleman

28th

THE BIRD OF NIGHT

A shadow is floating through the moonlight.
Its wings don't make a sound.
Its claws are long, its beak is bright.
Its eyes try all the corners of the night.

It calls and calls: all the air swells and heaves
And washes up and down like water.
The ear that listens to the owl believes
In death. The bat beneath the eaves,

The mouse beside the stone are still as death.
The owl's air washes them like water.
The owl goes back and forth inside the night,
And the night holds its breath.

Randall Jarrell

29th

MIDNIGHT VISITORS

Hedgehog comes snuffling
in his prickly coat,
scuffing the leaves for slugs.

Cat comes soft as a moth,
a shadow painted on the lawn
by moonlight.

Owl comes floating,
sits still as a cat on the wall,
watching, listening.

Mouse freezes under the leaves
on tiptoe paws,
quick eyes pin-bright,
hungry.

Irene Rawnsley

30th

THE PUMPKIN

One day I found two pumpkin seeds.
I planted one and pulled the weeds.
It sprouted roots and a big, long vine.
A pumpkin grew; I called it mine.
The pumpkin was quite round and fat.
(I really am quite proud of that.)
But there is something I'll admit
That has me worried just a bit.
I ate the other seed, you see.
Now will it grow inside of me?

(I'm so relieved since I have found
That pumpkins only grow in the ground!)

Anonymous

31st

THE BAT

By day the bat is cousin to the mouse.
He likes the attic of an aging house.

His fingers make a hat about his head.
His pulse beat is so slow we think him dead.

He loops in crazy figures half the night
Among the trees that face the corner light.

But when he brushes up against a screen,
We are afraid of what our eyes have seen;

For something is amiss or out of place
When mice with wings can wear a human face.

Theodore Roethke

NOVEMBER

1st

THE NIGHT WILL NEVER STAY

The night will never stay,
    The night will still go by,
Though with a million stars
    You pin it to the sky,
Though you bind it with the blowing wind
    And buckle it with the moon,
The night will slip away
    Like sorrow or a tune.

Eleanor Farjeon

2nd

SKYSCRAPERS

Do skyscrapers ever grow tired
Of holding themselves up high?
Do they ever shiver on frosty nights
With their tops against the sky?

Do they feel lonely sometimes
Because they have grown so tall?
Do they ever wish they could lie right down
And never get up at all?

Rachel Field

3rd

FOX

After dark
    when the cars park
        and the streets are quiet
Fox comes
loping calmly over the wall.

He strolls
    along the pavement
        and
          across the road
  with his long nose,
    sharp ears
      and his feathery brush of a tail,
flows like water through the shadows and hard
spaces.

He goes alone.
This is his place
    these trails of smells,
      the bins and bags that are his pickings
    the yards and parks,
      back alleys and the hollows under cars.

If we pass by he turns and with one look
    reminds us
      that we've only borrowed it.

Kathy Henderson

4th

AUTUMN FIRES

In the other gardens
    And all up the vale,
From the autumn bonfires
    See the smoke trail!

Pleasant summer over
    And all the summer flowers,
The red fire blazes,
    The grey smoke towers.

Sing a song of seasons!
    Something bright in all!
Flowers in the summer,
    Fires in the fall!

Robert Louis Stevenson

5th

Fires are flaming,
Flickering, flashing,
Full of fury,
Full of fancy.

Anonymous

6th

NOVEMBER NIGHT

Listen . . .
With faint dry sound,
Like steps of passing ghosts,
The leaves, frost-crisp'd, break from the trees
And fall.

Adelaide Crapsey

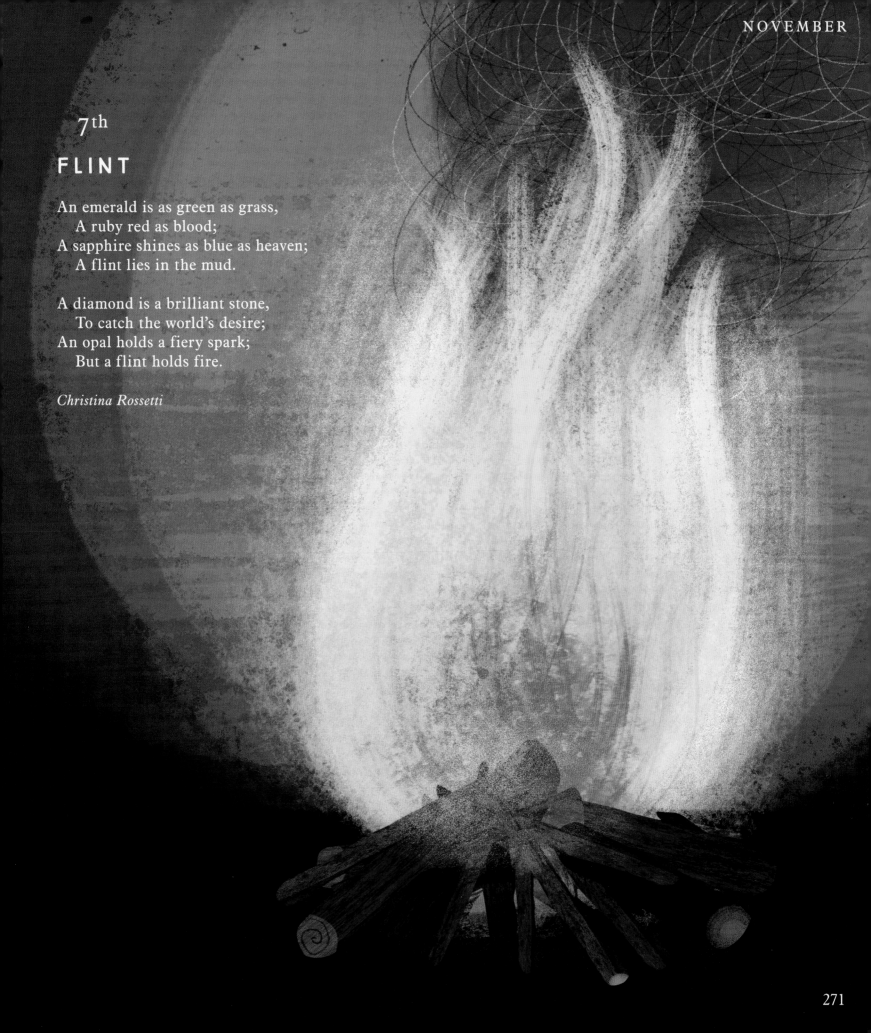

7th

FLINT

An emerald is as green as grass,
    A ruby red as blood;
A sapphire shines as blue as heaven;
    A flint lies in the mud.

A diamond is a brilliant stone,
    To catch the world's desire;
An opal holds a fiery spark;
    But a flint holds fire.

Christina Rossetti

8th

WEATHER REPORT

Pinging rain
stinging sleet
tonight.

Frost at dawn,
bright
sun in the morning.

Ice-bearing trees,
a glass
orchard,
blinking
sunwinking.

A noonwind will
pass,
harvesting the brittle crop,
crashing
clinking.

Lilian Moore

9th

AUTUMN

I love the fitful gust that shakes
   The casement all the day,
And from the glossy elm tree takes
   The faded leaves away,
Twirling them by the windowpane
With thousand others down the lane.

I love to see the shaking twig
   Dance till shut of eve,
The sparrow on the cottage rig,
   Whose chirp would make believe
That Spring was just now flirting by
In Summer's lap with flowers to lie.

I love to see the cottage smoke
   Curl upwards through the trees;
The pigeons nestled round the cote
   On November days like these;
The cock upon the dunghill crowing,
The mill sails on the heath a-going.

John Clare

10th

WEATHER OR NOT

The rain that was expected tomorrow
came today.
So the weather is now a day early.

Just think!
If the weather is running 24 hours ahead
what will happen on the Last Day?

Obviously,
having all been used up
there will be no weather.

Spooky, eh?

Roger McGough

11th

THE FOG

Slowly, the fog,
Hunch-shouldered with a grey face,
Arms wide, advances,
Fingertips touching the way
Past the dark houses
And dark gardens of roses.
Up the short street from the harbour,
Slowly the fog,
Seeking, seeking;
Arms wide, shoulders hunched,
Searching, searching.
Out through the streets to the fields,
Slowly, the fog —
A blind man hunting the moon.

F. R. McCreary

12th

FOG IN NOVEMBER

Fog in November, trees have no heads,
Streams only sound, walls suddenly stop
Halfway up hills, the ghost of a man spreads
Dung on dead fields for next year's crop.
I cannot see my hand before my face,
My body does not seem to be my own,
The world becomes a far-off, foreign place,
People are strangers, houses silent, unknown.

Leonard Clark

13th

WINTER SONG

The feathers of the reed
Are lying on the ground
And the quails are perched on the pines.

Southern Paiute song,
translated by John Wesley Powell

15th

THE STORM CROWN

It rains on the mountains
It rains on the mountains
A white crown encircles the mountain

Southern Paiute song,
translated by John Wesley Powell

14th

PINE TREE TOPS

In the blue night
frost haze, the sky glows
with the moon
pine tree tops
bend snow-blue, fade
into sky, frost, starlight.
The creak of boots.
Rabbit tracks, deer tracks,
what do we know.

Gary Snyder

16th

SIGHTED

Against the steel-grey
thunderous
tight-as-a-drum-skin
threatening sky,
I watch a brilliant
pure white
feathered wild-goose
dazzlingly fly.

John Mole

17th

SPACE POEM

The sun is like
a gold balloon

the moon
a silver pearl

the earth is like
a marble blue

the milky way
a creamy swirl.

If stars are like
those little boats

afloat a sea
of night

the dark is when
a hand comes down

and switches
off the light!

James Carter

18th

THE BLACKBIRD

In the far corner
close by the swings
every morning
a blackbird sings.

His bill's so yellow
his coat's so black
that he makes a fellow
whistle back.

Ann my daughter
thinks that he
sings for us two
especially.

Humbert Wolfe

19th

Dappled sunlight on
blue and gold feathers — birds dance
around the peanuts.

Alison Hunt

20th

A bitter morning:
sparrows sitting together
without any necks.

J. W. Hackett

21st

TURKEY TIME

Thanksgiving Day will soon be here;
It comes around but once a year.
If I could only have my way,
We'd have Thanksgiving every day!

Anonymous

22nd

THANKSGIVING

The year has turned its circle,
The seasons come and go.
The harvest is all gathered in
And chilly north winds blow.
Orchards have shared their treasures,
The fields, their yellow grain.
So open wide the doorway—
Thanksgiving comes again!

Anonymous

23rd

WINDY NIGHTS

Whenever the moon and stars are set,
  Whenever the wind is high,
All night long in the dark and wet,
  A man goes riding by.
Late in the night when the fires are out,
Why does he gallop and gallop about?

Whenever the trees are crying aloud,
  And ships are tossed at sea,
By, on the highway, low and loud,
  By at the gallop goes he.
By at the gallop he goes, and then
By he comes back at the gallop again.

Robert Louis Stevenson

24th

LIGHTSHIPS

All night long when the wind is high
Nnn nnn nnnn
The lightships moan and moan to the sky
Nnn nnn nnnn.

Their foghorns whine when the mist runs free
Nnn nnn nnnn
Warning the men on the ships at sea
Nnn nnn nnnn.

Clive Sansom

25th

THAT STORMY NIGHT

That stormy night
when the wind moaned like a wolf
and bent the trees, and shook the house
I wondered if it could blow the stars away.

What then — if their glittering dust
lay among the fallen leaves next day
crystals and splinters in the morning light?
I'd sweep them up and put them in a box

and bring them home to you. You'd say
*Nonsense. What you see up there
is light that's millions of years away
you know that, don't you?*

Yes. I know. But still
I'd shake my box of stardust
hold it tight
knowing the wind had blown the stars away

that stormy night.

Berlie Doherty

26th

THUNDER AND LIGHTNING

Blood punches through every vein
As lightning strips the windowpane.

Under its flashing whip, a white
Village leaps to light.

On tubs of thunder, fists of rain
Slog it out of sight again.

Blood punches the heart with fright
As rain belts the village night.

James Kirkup

27th

BIG SWIMMING

Rain on the high prairies,
In dusk of autumnal hills;
Under the creaking saddle
My cheerless pony plods . . .

Down where the obscure water
Lapping the lithe willows
Sunders the chilling plain—
Rusty-hearted and travel-worn—
We set our bodies
To the November flood.

The farther shore is a cloud
Beyond midnight . . .

Big swimming.

Edwin Ford Piper

28th

NIGHT SOUNDS

When I lie in bed
I think I can hear
The stars being switched on
I think I can.

And I think I can hear
The moon
Breathing.

But I have to be still.
So still.
All the house is sleeping.
Except for me.

Then I think I can hear it.

Berlie Doherty

29th

SILVER

Slowly, silently, now the moon
Walks the night in her silver shoon;
This way, and that, she peers, and sees
Silver fruit upon silver trees;
One by one the casements catch
Her beams beneath the silvery thatch;
Couched in his kennel, like a log,
With paws of silver sleeps the dog;
From their shadowy cote the white breasts peep
Of doves in a silver-feathered sleep;
A harvest mouse goes scampering by,
With silver claws, and silver eye;
And moveless fish in the water gleam,
By silver reeds in a silver stream.

Walter de la Mare

30th

WHITE SOUND

When rain
whispers
it is snow.

Julie O'Callaghan

DECEMBER

1st

DORMOUSE

"Now Winter is coming,"
The dormouse said,
"I must be thinking
Of going to bed."
So he curled himself up
As small as he could,
And went fast asleep
As a dormouse should.

Lilian McCrea

2nd

SNOW

No breath of wind,
No gleam of sun —
Still the white snow
Whirls softly down —
Twig and bough
And blade and thorn.
All in an icy
Quiet, forlorn.
Whispering, rustling,
Through the air,
On sill and stone,
Roof — everywhere,
It heaps its powdery
Crystal flakes,
Of every tree
A mountain makes;
Till pale and faint
At shut of day,
Stoops from the West
One wintry ray.
And, feathered in fire,
Where ghosts the moon,
A robin shrills
His lonely tune.

Walter de la Mare

3rd

QUESTIONING FACES

The winter owl banked just in time to pass
And save herself from breaking window glass.
And her wings straining suddenly aspread
Caught color from the last of evening red
In a display of underdown and quill
To glassed-in children at the windowsill.

Robert Frost

4th

RED SKY
AT NIGHT

Red sky at night,
Shepherd's delight;
Red sky in the morning,
Shepherd's warning.

Anonymous

5th

THE NORTH WIND DOTH BLOW (EXTRACT)

The north wind doth blow
And we shall have snow,
And what will poor robin do then, poor thing?
   He'll sit in a barn,
      And keep himself warm,
And hide his head under his wing, poor thing!

The north wind doth blow
And we shall have snow,
And what will the dormouse do then, poor thing?
   Rolled up like a ball,
      In his nest snug and small,
He'll sleep till warm weather comes in, poor thing!

The north wind doth blow
And we shall have snow,
And what will the children do then, poor things?
   When lessons are done,
      They'll skip, jump, and run,
Until they have made themselves warm, poor things!

Anonymous

6th

THE MUSIC OF THE WIND

The wind
　　makes LOUD music.
It roars above the rooftops,
it drums beneath the floor,
it howls around the gable-end
and rat-a-tats the door.

The wind
　　makes quiet music.
It whistles down the chimney,
it tiptoes through a tree,
it hums against the window-pane,
and whispers tunes to me.

Wes Magee

7th

WINTER TREES

Aren't you cold and won't you freeze,
With branches bare, you winter trees?
You've thrown away your summer shift,
Your autumn gold has come adrift.

Dearie me, you winter trees,
What strange behaviour, if you please!
In summer you could wear much less,
But come the winter—you undress!

Zoltán Zelk, translated by George Szirtes

8th

THE SEA

Deep glass-green seas
chew rocks
with their green-glass jaws.
But little waves
creep in
and nibble softly at the sand.

Lilith Norman

9th

THE TIDE RISES,
THE TIDE FALLS

The tide rises, the tide falls,
The twilight darkens, the curlew calls;
Along the sea-sands damp and brown
The traveler hastens toward the town,
    And the tide rises, the tide falls.

Darkness settles on roofs and walls,
But the sea, the sea in the darkness calls;
The little waves, with their soft, white hands,
Efface the footprints in the sands,
    And the tide rises, the tide falls.

The morning breaks; the steeds in their stalls
Stamp and neigh, as the hostler calls;
The day returns, but nevermore
Returns the traveler to the shore,
    And the tide rises, the tide falls.

Henry Wadsworth Longfellow

10th

DAUGHTER
OF THE SEA

bog seeper
moss creeper
growing restless
getting steeper

trickle husher
swish and rusher
stone leaper
splash and gusher

foam flicker
mirror slicker
pebble pusher
boulder kicker

still pool
don't be fooled
shadow tricker
keeping cool

leap lunger
crash plunger
free fall
with thunder under

idle winder
youth behind her
little wonder
daily grinder

garbage binner
dump it in her
never mind her
dog's dinner

plastic bagger
old lagger
oil skinner
wharf nagger

cargo porter
weary water
tide dragger
long lost daughter

of the sea
the sea the sea
has caught her
up in its arms and set her free

Philip Gross

11th

KIT'S FIRST SNOW

His world had gone
Overnight—
Paths, tracks, known smells
All sunk
Under soft whiteness
That made him wince and sneeze.
Packed footmarks showed
Where the milkman had trod;
A second set, the postman's.
Kit, on flinching paws,
Quickstepped to the gate
In a dazzle of white.
Couldn't see where it ended
So stood up to stare,
Poised like a meerkat.

An exclamation in the snow—
Black kitten
In a white world.

Linda Newbery

12th

ONLY SNOW

Outside, the sky was almost brown.
The clouds were hanging low.
Then all of a sudden it happened:
The air was full of snow.

The children rushed to the windows.
The teacher let them go,
Though she teased them for their foolishness.
After all, it was only snow.

It was only snow that was falling,
Only out of the sky,
Only on to the turning earth
Before the blink of an eye.

What else could it do from up there,
But fall in the usual way?
It was only *weather*, really.
What else could you say?

The teacher sat at her desk
Putting ticks in a little row,
While the children stared through steamy glass
At the only snow.

Allan Ahlberg

13th

SUMMER AND WINTER

When a warm dawn brings
the sun to your eyes,
blink three times—
it's time to rise.

When cold winds whistle
around your head,
pull it under the blankets
and stay in bed.

Michael Dugan

14th

DRAGON SMOKE

Breathe and blow
white clouds
  with every puff.
It's cold today,
  cold enough
to see your breath.
Huff!
  Breathe dragon smoke
    today!

Lilian Moore

15th

THE RAIN HAS SILVER SANDALS

The rain has silver sandals
  For dancing in the spring,
And shoes with golden tassels
  For summer's frolicking.
Her winter boots have hobnails
  Of ice from heel to toe,
Which now and then she changes
  For moccasins of snow.

May Justus

16th

ALL DAY
SATURDAY

Let it sleet on Sunday,
Monday let it snow,
Let the mist on Tuesday
From the salt-sea flow.
Let it hail on Wednesday,
Thursday let it rain,
Let the wind on Friday
Blow a hurricane,
But Saturday, Saturday
Break fair and fine
And all day Saturday
Let the sun shine.

Charles Causley

17th

IF I COULD ONLY
TAKE HOME A
SNOWFLAKE

Snowflakes
like tiny
insects
drifting down.

Without a hum
they come,
Without a hum
they go

Snowflakes
like tiny
insects
drifting
down.

If only
I could take
one
home with me
to show
my friends
in the sun,
just for fun,
just for fun.

John Agard

18th

SNOWFLAKES

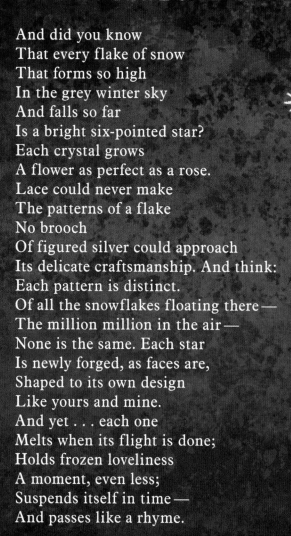

And did you know
That every flake of snow
That forms so high
In the grey winter sky
And falls so far
Is a bright six-pointed star?
Each crystal grows
A flower as perfect as a rose.
Lace could never make
The patterns of a flake
No brooch
Of figured silver could approach
Its delicate craftsmanship. And think:
Each pattern is distinct.
Of all the snowflakes floating there—
The million million in the air—
None is the same. Each star
Is newly forged, as faces are,
Shaped to its own design
Like yours and mine.
And yet . . . each one
Melts when its flight is done;
Holds frozen loveliness
A moment, even less;
Suspends itself in time—
And passes like a rhyme.

Clive Sansom

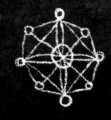

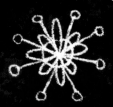

THE MONTHS

January desolate;
February dripping wet;
March wind ranges;
April changes;
Birds sing in tune
To flowers of May,
And sunny June
Brings longest day;
In scorched July
The storm-clouds fly
Lightning-torn;
August bears corn,
September fruit;
In rough October
Earth must disrobe her;
Stars fall and shoot
In keen November;
And night is long
And cold is strong
In bleak December.

Christina Rossetti

IN THE MOONLIGHT

We looked out of our bedroom at moonlight:
Now how could we go to sleep
When the world out there was as bright as day
And the snow was lying deep?

So we muffled up and out we went—
Nobody heard us go—
And we stood in the magic of moonlight
In a garden wrapped in snow.

Everything changed, enchanted:
Our garden seat a throne,
The bushes softly smothered,
The trees as white as bone.

For a while we could only look,
Held in a spell, but soon
We were shaping hard, cold snowballs
And throwing them at the moon.

Tomorrow: snowmen and snowfights
And clearing a track for the cars,
Treading it all into slush, but tonight
We snowballed the moon and stars.

Eric Finney

21st

WINTER

Winter crept
through the whispering wood,
hushing fir and oak;
crushed each leaf and froze each web —
but never a word he spoke.

Winter prowled
by the shivering sea,
lifting sand and stone;
nipped each limpet silently —
and then moved on.

Winter raced
down the frozen stream,
catching at his breath;
on his lips were icicles,
at his back was death.

Judith Nicholls

22nd

WINTER TREES

All the complicated details
of the attiring and
the disattiring are completed!
A liquid moon
moves gently among
the long branches.
Thus having prepared their buds
against a sure winter
the wise trees
stand sleeping in the cold.

William Carlos Williams

23rd

BE LIKE THE BIRD

Be like the bird, who
Resting in his flight
On a twig too slight
Feels it bend beneath him,
Yet sings
Knowing he has wings.

Victor Hugo

24th

AT NINE OF THE NIGHT
I OPENED MY DOOR

At nine of the night I opened my door
That stands midway between moor and moor,
And all around me, silver-bright,
I saw that the world had turned to white.

Thick was the snow on field and hedge
And vanished was the river-sedge,
Where winter skilfully had wound
A shining scarf without a sound.

And as I stood and gazed my fill
A stable-boy came down the hill.
With every step I saw him take
Flew at his heel a puff of flake.

His brow was whiter than the hoar,
A beard of freshest snow he wore,
And round about him, snowflake starred,
A red horse-blanket from the yard.

In a red cloak I saw him go,
His back was bent, his step was slow,
And as he laboured through the cold
He seemed a hundred winters old.

I stood and watched the snowy head,
The whiskers white, the cloak of red.
"A Merry Christmas!" I heard him cry.
"The same to you, old friend," said I.

Charles Causley

25th

THE HOLLY AND THE IVY (EXTRACT)

The holly and the ivy,
When they are both full grown,
Of all the trees that are in the wood,
The holly bears the crown.

O the rising of the sun,
And the running of the deer,
The playing of the merry organ,
Sweet singing in the choir.

Anonymous

26th

THE FALLOW DEER
AT THE LONELY HOUSE

One without looks in tonight
   Through the curtain-chink
From the sheet of glistening white;
One without looks in tonight
   As we sit and think
   By the fender-brink.

We do not discern those eyes
   Watching in the snow;
Lit by lamps of rosy dyes
We do not discern those eyes
   Wondering, aglow
   Four-footed, tiptoe.

Thomas Hardy

27th

THE PINES

The lofty pines
The tops of the lofty pines
The lofty pines
Are swaying with the winds

Southern Paiute song,
translated by John Wesley Powell

28th

AMULET

Inside the wolf's fang, the mountain of heather.
Inside the mountain of heather, the wolf's fur.
Inside the wolf's fur, the ragged forest.
Inside the ragged forest, the wolf's foot.
Inside the wolf's foot, the stony horizon.
Inside the stony horizon, the wolf's tongue.
Inside the wolf's tongue, the doe's tears.
Inside the doe's tears, the frozen swamp.
Inside the frozen swamp, the wolf's blood.
Inside the wolf's blood, the snow wind.
Inside the snow wind, the wolf's eye.
Inside the wolf's eye, the North Star.
Inside the North Star, the wolf's fang.

Ted Hughes

29th

THE FOUR CORNERS OF THE UNIVERSE

You will be running to the four corners of
   the universe;
To where the land meets the big water;
To where the sky meets the land;
To where the home of winter is;
To the home of rain.
Run!
Be strong.
For you are the mother of a people.

Mescalero Apache song,
translated by Claire R. Farrer

30th

I HEARD A BIRD SING

I heard a bird sing
In the dark of December
A magical thing
And sweet to remember.

"We are nearer to spring
Than we were in September,"
I heard a bird sing
In the dark of December.

Oliver Herford

31st

KEEP A POEM
IN YOUR POCKET

Keep a poem in your pocket
and a picture in your head
and you'll never feel lonely
at night when you're in bed.

The little poem will sing to you
the little picture bring to you
a dozen dreams to dance to you
at night when you're in bed.

So—
Keep a picture in your pocket
and a poem in your head
and you'll never feel lonely
at night when you're in bed.

Beatrice Schenk de Regniers

INDEX OF POETS

INDEX OF POEMS

INDEX OF FIRST LINES

COPYRIGHT ACKNOWLEDGMENTS